Also by Caroline Alexander

One Dry Season
The Way to Xanadu

BATTLE'S END

BATTLE'S END

A SEMINOLE FOOTBALL
TEAM REVISITED

Caroline Alexander

 ALFRED A. KNOPF   NEW YORK   1995

This Is a Borzoi Book Published by Alfred A. Knopf, Inc.

Grateful acknowledgment is made to Thomas Wright for permission to
reprint the Florida State "Fight Song," words by Doug Alley, music
by Thomas Wright.

Photographs are courtesy of F.S.U. Sports Information.

ISBN 0-679-41901-2

LC 95-81630

Manufactured in the United States of America
First Edition

To My Mother

and all the mothers
mentioned in this book

FLORIDA STATE "FIGHT SONG"

You got to fight, fight, fight for F.S.U.
You got to scalp 'em, Seminoles.
You got to win, win, win, win, win this game,
And roll on down to make those goals.
For F.S.U. is on the warpath now
And at the battle's end she's great.
So fight, fight, fight, fight to victory,
You Seminoles from Florida State.

(*Yell*)
F-L-O-R-I-D-A S-T-A-T-E
Florida State! Florida State! Florida State!

(*Repeat chorus*)

Contents

BATTLE'S END

IN THE SHADOW
OF THE COLISEUM

I grew up hearing the sound of tom-toms pounding in the night. This was in Tallahassee, Florida, where we lived on an otherwise quiet, tree-shaded street, less than a mile distant from the Florida State University football stadium. Florida State, as the world knows, is home of the Florida State Seminoles, a composite tribe distinguished by the attributes of a number of real and fondly imagined peoples. Sammy Seminole, the school mascot, rides a white charger but wears a jacket of the boldly striped appliqué that characterizes genuine Seminole workmanship. He and his fans smear their faces with Apache war paint, and in the old days the sound of tom-toms pounding used to be broadcast over a loudspeaker system into the Florida night. Recently, a delegation of real Seminoles registered their indignation at this fraudulent and disrespectful use of their name, but their stand was undercut by their own chief, who indicated that he was proud to be associated with the number-one collegiate football team in the nation.

Although as a child I knew that the sound of the drums came from the stadium, to me, lying rigid in the night, the noise was unspeakably sinister. In the darkness, I could too easily visualize a raucous mob swarming from the stadium and heading inexorably for the exact street where we lived. In my night vision the faces of this advancing throng were shadowy, indistinct—but they were definitely not Indian; if pressed, I would have said they most resembled those large and boisterous white men one saw on the day of a big game, filing over Pensacola Bridge toward the stadium with beer mugs in their hands.

This identification of my fellow citizens and townsfolk as hostile savages says much about the nature of my childhood. Both my parents are English and had first come to North Florida in the mid-1950s. They had lived briefly in Gainesville, where I was born, then moved to Jamaica, in the West Indies, my sister's birthplace, before settling in Tallahassee in 1960. For them, I believe, Tallahassee was as exotic and foreign as Jamaica—although perhaps in some ways less civilized, in view of the fact that Jamaica, as a former British colony, was in many ways more familiarly English. I don't think either of them had any intention of returning to England, nor, particularly on my mother's part, was life marked by any nostalgia for their transatlantic home. Nonetheless, although they were outgoing and sociable and admired much of what they encountered in the brave new world of North Florida, my parents never lost their sense of being foreigners in an alien culture. When I lived in Africa years later, I recognized the same unreflective attitudes in the resident expatriates which I had observed years earlier at home: an affectionate appreciation for the majority population around them, but absolutely no conception of the possibility of living as they did.

This rather easygoing "apartness" from mainstream southern culture was exacerbated with my parents' divorce. They had both immigrated to the States on a limited-term visa that required repeated, biannual petitions for its extension. My father, characteristically complacent that this ritual would continue indefinitely, had come to regard it as a mere formality and was thus genuinely indignant when one year his "pro forma" application was refused, compelling him to return at short notice and kicking hard to Jamaica. As a last bid for reinstatement, he claimed the necessity of being around to help raise his American-born daughter—myself—but in view of the fact that he did not pay child support, this plea was unconvincing. The Immigration Office proved to be more sympathetic to my mother, but the Department of Labor was stickier. And when her Certificate of Work application was turned down, she announced to the Labor Office in Washington that she was prepared to return to England—but would be leaving her American daughter on their doorstep. Successfully awarded the necessary papers within a week, she enrolled at Florida State as an undergraduate student, acquiring foreign-student status by so doing and with it the right to work, for a dollar an hour, at a student job, and thus she joined the ranks of women who must carry single-handedly the burden of their small worlds upon their shoulders. In those days, although not so very long ago, single mothers were not looked upon with much sympathy in the South. At her divorce proceedings, my mother was awarded inadequate financial support, the judge noting that she was "still attractive" and would be able to find another husband. But even this minimal support was erratically delivered and eventually evaporated, so that for many years her student job was our only source of income.

Despite these difficulties, my mother was determined not to return to England, and her ongoing battle with the Department of Labor, which prevented the Immigration Office from granting an immigration visa, loomed larger in our lives than any other factor, including finances. Every action was a potential pitfall, a chance to draw the vigilant attention of immigration officials upon our heads, and life for my sister, Joanna, and me was full of arcane instructions. We were told, for example, that we must never ride in a car with anyone, licensed or not, under the age of twenty-one, as to do so—according to my mother—was highly illegal. She was terrified of accidents, but not only for the obvious reasons. An accident could land one in the hospital, and the cost for treatment in an American hospital, she had been told, would be impossibly expensive. If treated at a hospital, therefore, we would in all likelihood be unable to pay, a fact that would be relayed to the immigration authorities, who would deport us. Similarly, as we got older, we were told that it was illegal to reverse a car in a parking lot and, although not strictly against the law, *wrong* to ride in the backseat.

With so many minefields to negotiate, it was perhaps unsurprising that my sister and I tended to stay close to home, where the rules were clearly known. The fact that our peers seemed unmindful of all these hazards only emphasized the legitimacy of our mother's point of view: of course *they* didn't worry; they were Americans.

Our assimilation was also curtailed by bare financial realities. Even before my parents had divorced, we had never owned a television, and after the divorce such an unnecessary item was no longer feasible, even if it had been desirable. We could not afford to buy record albums, nor did we go very often to movies. My father, who had learned at an early stage of the game that an Oxford-educated English gentleman could gain enormous mileage among hospitable southern women, and whose Englishness, therefore, was more practiced, had never bought a local newspaper, preferring to have the London *Times* sent conspicuously from England, and after he left, the subscription eventually ran out and was never replaced. Neither was his shortwave radio, by which he used to get the BBC news from London. In these important respects, then, we were effectively cut off from the mainstream culture of our peers.

I have always been of an essentially reclusive nature. To the first proper birthday party I ever had, I invited only my favorite stuffed animals, and photographs taken of this festive occasion show me looking highly pleased with the proceedings. I was also something of a snob, preferring the elite company of a good book to most of the ordinary people about me, and I spent all my spare time reading. The circumstances of our family's political and financial woes, then, did not so much isolate me as they did cater to already strong isolationist tendencies. Furthermore, life in our house seemed more amusing than anything I observed going on outside. My mother, my sister, and I were always discussing books, plans and projects, possibilities of travel; on two occasions my mother took yearlong student jobs abroad, ensuring that we lived in Italy and Holland, from where on both occasions we traveled extensively. Looking out from inside our house, life seemed endlessly exciting.

By contrast, the world immediately beyond our garden, other parts of Tallahassee, I found alien, unintriguing, and at times intimidating. While I was aware that there were normal, orthodox ways of doing most things, I was never sure I knew them, and there was no telling when or how such ignorance might be exposed. A social science teacher in high school once badgered me in front of the class by asking if I would prefer to eat red snapper or squid. This interrogation had arisen because he had somehow heard that I'd said I didn't like seafood—the fact I kept obstinately repeating by way of answering him.

"Do you mean to tell me," he concluded in a kind of white-hot rage, "that after all the years you have lived in this country you would as soon have what they eat in Communist China as in the United States of America?" ("I intend to break her spirit," the same teacher once told my mother, on one of the numerous occasions she had to come to the school. "Good luck," she had replied. "Better men than you have tried.")

It would perhaps have been easier for me had I been a Hindu or a Hottentot, recognized on sight as being manifestly and truly foreign, and thus expected to speak and behave in peculiar ways. As it was, I found all encounters with strangers, such as salespeople in shops, deeply uncomfortable. Aware that even in the most casual circumstances there existed spoken and behavioral codes, like those exchanged between birds of the same species, which identified the user as a bona fide customer/citizen, I rehearsed for every encounter the way one practices phrase-book expressions in a foreign language.

The only place outside of home where I felt entirely comfortable was school. Inexplicably so, because there were many reasons—our English accents, the way we dressed, the fact that we had to have free school meals—why my sister and I should have felt awkward. We were both good students, however, and genuinely liked learning, and so perhaps in important ways were more confident than many of our peers. But even here I knew that it was generally recognized, by students and teachers alike, that I did not entirely fit, did not know—let alone abide by—certain social rules. One circumstance serves to illustrate the almost unthinkable extent to which I lived beyond the southern social pale: the only extracurricular activity I had any real interest in was going to basketball games, not because I particularly liked basketball but because I had friends on the team and friends who went to the games. On these occasions, there were never many other white faces in the watching crowd, and those that were white tended to be grouped together. Several times, on leaving the auditorium at the end of a game, I heard friends of my friends from the rival school comment on my presence. "She's not white, she's English," I heard in my defense on more than one occasion.

Tallahassee was, when my family first arrived, a small university town of fewer than fifty thousand inhabitants. We were always told that Tallahassee was more akin to the Deep South, to southern Georgia, than to other parts of Florida, and it was certainly true that my parents didn't find the landscape they had expected based upon the rumors and reports of Florida that had made their way to England. There were the famous beaches of white sand, to be sure, but also dipping hills and woods and throughout all the surrounding countryside, as well as in town itself, the great, spreading, ancient live oak trees. They had expected perpetual summer, but found that there were four distinct, if abbreviated, seasons that changed the color of the luxuriant foliage and brought killing frosts at night. Spring was not comparable to anything they had previously known: balmy, breezy, sensuous, a tangle of purple wisteria and dogwood, gardenias and blazing azaleas, and always the heavy, primeval ropes of Spanish moss. Tallahassee was in many respects still a small town then. My mother could never get over the fact that when she first moved into our new house, neighbors had come over to greet her, bringing gifts of homemade food. In England, one's arrival in a new neighborhood would have been scrutinized in a kind of outraged silence from behind carefully held net curtains.

In downtown Tallahassee—around the courthouse and the post office with its Old World mural depicting the arrival in Florida of the Spanish conquistadores, along the streets that ran off from the little town green where the May Queen was crowned each year—stood white wooden houses dating from the late nineteenth century. Monroe Street, the main artery through the downtown area, had one movie theater, a drugstore with a soda counter, the old Floridian Hotel, and Morrison's Cafeteria, one of the town's few restaurants. Today, this downtown area is essentially dead, all business having moved out to the malls, and the old white houses are attorneys' offices. Nonetheless, even now there are longtime Tallahassee residents who remember when Monroe Street was an unpaved dirt track.

Off Monroe, College Avenue leads straight to the gates of the Florida State campus. Established in 1857 as the Seminary West of the Suwannee, it became the Florida State College for Women from 1909 to 1947, at which time it became coeducational. The older buildings, attractive in their redbricked, gabled, earnest collegiate optimism, and the ancient and majestic moss-hung oaks near the southern entrance once composed the entire campus. Occasionally, one still runs into graduates of this earlier institution, resolute and quietly dynamic women who can recite Virgil and Rupert Brooke by heart.

At the time my parents first arrived, the university's total enrollment was well under ten thousand students. The campus was small, safe, and easy to negotiate, and my sister and I spent much of our childhood availing ourselves of its various facilities—

diving for the change that fell out of the pockets of other swimmers in the big outdoor pool, going to the student-priced films in the old auditorium, browsing for hours in the school library. We lived within walking distance of the campus—although to my mother all distances were walking distances for children—about a mile up the hill from the football stadium, a lumbering, uncouth structure painted mustard yellow, whose every beam and underpinning was exposed to harsh view, so that one felt that it was always under construction.

In 1960, the year we arrived in Tallahassee, Doak Campbell Stadium, as it is so named, had a seating capacity of twenty-one thousand, ample for a team that was essentially ranked nowhere. Florida State's opening game that year was against George Washington; other teams played in the same season were Florida, Mississippi, Georgia, Richmond, Virginia Tech, Kentucky, the Citadel, Mississippi Southern, and Houston. The Seminoles had closed the year before with a 4-5-1 record, and head coach Bill Peterson noted with dogged professional optimism that the 1960 team should be an improvement over last year's squad, "principally because our younger players have a year of experience." In spite of these not particularly compelling statistics, each home game was played to a nearly full house—in those days, in any case, it was really only the outcome of the Florida game that mattered. The women in garnet-and-gold suits, heels, and corsages, the men more casual but still decorous, the fans would stream toward the stadium down over the Pensacola Street Bridge that formed an overpass across the entrance to the stadium parking lot. There were tailgate picnics and pregame parties, powwows and parades, and tom-toms pounding in the night.

Social bonds, as anthropologists know, are formed by participation in traditional tribal rites, and the fact that we as virtual foreigners were unable to comprehend or take seriously the pervasive devotion to football marked my family, as much as any single factor, as members of an essentially alien tribe. My father's pose was to pooh-pooh American football, comparing it unfavorably to rugby, which, incidentally, he did not play. The helmets, the padding, the frequent substitutions—in his practiced charming English way he hinted at the unthinkable: that American football was for sissies. My mother, who had been a champion competitive swimmer in England, had little time for spectator sports of any kind, and most definitely not for those in which women stood on the sidelines and cheered for men. As for me, I had never seen football even on television, but had little desire to find out for myself what all the uproar down the road was about. I resented the cars that were parked on our street on the day of a game, I resented the noise, and could imagine nothing more miserable than sitting in the cold late-autumn air, surrounded by yelling strangers. In the football players themselves we had no interest, and with one exception I could not have named any member of the Seminole squad of any year. The lone exception was Ivory Joe Hunter, because with a name like that, whatever you end up doing you are surely worth remembering.

At the age of about fifteen, I had my only head-on encounter with a group of actual players. In fact, the whole team was stabled not far down the road from us, about halfway from our house to the campus. The football office had taken over an apartment complex on a high embankment overlooking the stadium. This complex, greatly expanded, is today called the Burt Reynolds Apartments after its famous primary benefactor, but in earlier years it was called, by chance or cynical intent, the Apartment Casa del Gatto. For many years, students walking to campus cut through the parking lot at the back of these buildings to some rough steps leading down the embankment to the road and the stadium parking lot below.

Joanna and I had walked this back way to high school for years, but would never have thought of venturing to the front of the apartments proper. One day, however, our pet tomcat, Beowulf, went missing, and my mother, Joanna, and I conducted a lengthy search throughout the neighborhood, gradually and despairingly extending it farther and farther from the house as the hours passed. I ended up at the bottom of Belle Vue Road facing the football apartments, by now crying with the realization that Beowulf was gone (and, indeed, we never found him). Having searched the back of the apartments, I wandered into the front, checking under bushes.

"Whatch you want?" The shout came from the balcony, and I looked up to see a crowd of men looking down and laughing. In tears, with all defenses gone, I called back that I was looking for my black cat. There was a wave of laughter; every face looking down, I then realized, was black.

"A black cat? You came to the right place, baby!"

In late 1977, I left Tallahassee and F.S.U. to go to university in England, and when I returned, in 1981, I discovered that a momentous change had taken place—Bobby Bowden was now head football coach and only the year before had led the Seminoles to a highly satisfying 10-2-0 season. In fact, I had briefly overlapped with the Bowden tenure before departing for England and remembered the much-publicized and acrimonious buyout of ex-coach Darryl Mudra's contract by the alumni boosters (Mudra went on to coach the Sopchoppy Yellowjackets). Bowden had therefore been safely ensconced at F.S.U. before I left, but the full test of his particular mettle was made while I was away, during which time he had had the opportunity to field his own recruits and forge his own distinctive program.

Before I had gone to England, football was a topic that could easily be ignored or avoided if one had no interest in it. Bowden-era football, so it seemed, was something about which everyone had an opinion, whether good or ill, and was therefore inescapable. Football in Tallahassee was now no longer a mere social institution; it was a force, a kind of groundswell of renewed optimism, like that drummed up in tented roadside revivals. Bowden's seasons had not been spectacular, but he had captured the faith of the people he served, and everybody now felt that we—Tallahasseeans as well as those associated specifically with F.S.U.—were bound for reflected glory. Bowden himself was to be seen everywhere: in the Tallahassee *Democrat*, on the local television station selling cars, preaching at his Baptist church. In the eyes of his community and, most important, of the boosters and alumni, Saint Bobby, as he had been dubbed, could do no wrong, and everyone now seemed to be waiting patiently for destiny to happen. Florida State had had a Nobel Prize–winning physicist (Paul Dirac); it had one of the very few superconducting linear accelerators in the world; it had even had me, its only Rhodes scholar. But not until now, after all those empty years and decades, was it on its way to having a powerhouse football program and thus to becoming, at last, a real university.

I had returned to Tallahassee for a very specific purpose: I had come to train full-time in preparation for the U.S. Modern Pentathlon National Championships, to be held in the summer of 1982 and at which I hoped to win a place on the World Team. This requires some explanation. Modern pentathlon is an eccentric sport, well known in Europe and particularly in the former Eastern-bloc countries, but mostly notable for its obscurity in the United States. As its name implies, it is a composite of five events—épée fencing, stadium show jumping, swimming, pistol shooting, and cross-country running. In the ancient Olympic Games, the pentathlon (which included wrestling, javelin throwing, and sprinting) had been the centerpiece event, its skills chosen to reflect those of the ideal warrior. When the modern games were reinstituted, in 1896, a new pentathlon event was devised in the same spirit—although most people today would probably feel that its constituent skills better characterize a Napoleonic courier than an ideal warrior.

The United States Modern Pentathlon National and Olympic Training Center is situated, for reasons that remain unclear to everyone, in the Fort Sam Houston Army Base in San Antonio, Texas, and aspiring pentathletes are admitted to the center on the basis of their combined run/swim ability. Before I left for England, I had been instrumental in having this traditionally military sport opened to women, and in 1978, taking a summer leave from England, I had been the alternate for the women's World Team. In England, I had only been able to train very irregularly, and it was my hope that now, three years later, with six months of full-time preparation behind me, I could make a successful bid for a World Team place.

I should admit at the outset that this dream was never remotely realized, and for reasons that I have come to find instructive. In the eventual national competition, I rode for a perfect 1,100 points, had one of the highest run/swim combinations, fenced poorly, but not disastrously—and scored nearly zero points in pistol marksmanship. This was the same event that had lost me a team place, and even a championship title, in 1978.

Pistol shooting, alone of the pentathlon events, does not depend upon physical strength. There are many physical factors— even down to breathing—that one must control, but it is essentially a mental art. In all sports, I showed natural ability but no strictly competitive skills whatsoever; I was the kind of athlete who was more likely to swim a faster time in practice than on the day of a big meet. This inability to summon and control competitive instincts at the specifically critical moment is brutally but accurately called "choking." And while physical ability alone could carry me through to a limited extent in other events, there is no way to fake psychological toughness in an almost purely mental sport like target shooting.

In pentathlon, turning targets are used. One begins by taking up position with the pistol held pointing downward and only the target edges visible. The target suddenly turns so that it is facing the shooting booths, then turns edgewise again: the competitor has three seconds between the turns to raise the pistol, align it, and fire. In all, a total of twenty bullets are fired in four intervals of groups of five.

During practice sessions, and even during the warm-up

rounds immediately prior to the competition, I did not shoot badly. I felt relaxed and prepared even as I stepped into the competitive booth. But as the first target turned and I instinctively raised my gun, I beheld an unexpected and amazing sight: the gun was shaking, twisting back and forth so wildly that there seemed no chance of steadying, let alone aligning, it. I felt no panic, indeed almost no personal attachment to this phenomenon, and yet I identified the hand holding the gun as my own. I dared not lose a chance to score, and so I fired, but it was a question now of hitting the target at all, not of aiming for the black or the bull's-eye. And again for the second shot; and for the third . . . and finally the competition was over.

"Girl," said the sergeant, who was helping score the event, "you would have done better just throwing rocks at this paper."

How does one take charge at the instant of danger? How assess the situation, summon the energy to focus on one's weakness, fight it, harness the moment, wrestle it down, come through? I was later helpfully told that I lacked competitive experience, and this was to some degree true. I had briefly been on a gymnastic team when I was in high school, but my fear of an accident (hospital bills, reports to immigration) prevented me from attempting anything even vaguely risky. I had swum on a city team for some years, which I enjoyed; at least, I enjoyed the practices but, as was also the case with gymnastics, avoided the competitive meets. I disliked being uprooted from the safe routine of my home for the away trips, and also felt that the inevitable expense—registration fees, gas, motels, and restaurant meals—couldn't really be justified. I did sports with no sense of urgency, without ever feeling, even in a national championship, that anything of real consequence was at stake. More seriously, I was cursed with the squeamish bone-deep belief, perhaps a legacy of my British birthright, that it was undignified to try too hard—or at any rate to be *seen* to be trying too hard. Nonetheless, the upshot of all of this was that from a very early stage I have always had a healthy regard for those athletes who can perform under pressure and deliver the goods. To be able to do so manifests a special kind of unshakable mental power—the kind of intelligence that turns the tide of battles, that is coolheaded under fire.

All of this lay in the future, however, when I returned to Tallahassee in the late fall of 1981 and set out to find an evening job that would enable me to train full-time during the day. A friend at the university suggested tutoring for the athletic department—football per se was not mentioned—which sounded ideal. I went for an interview and was hired and told to start that same evening.

During my own student days at F.S.U., I had taken a history course given by an elderly, mild-mannered, and much-esteemed professor, who one day shared an anecdote with our class. He had recently been strongly taken to task by the football office for publicly insulting one of the players. The incident was much on his mind, and as he spoke his pale blue eyes blinked at us nervously at the mere memory of the ordeal. He had protested that he had never insulted anybody, but the football representative stood firm; he knew the facts and Professor Hare had called one of his boys "a reptile."

"I think I said 'gladiator,' " Professor Hare had gently asserted when he at last figured out where the misunderstanding lay. This was a dangerous word to bandy about, down here in alligator territory.

I am sure that jokes and anecdotes about student-athletes were rife, but this is the only such incident I can recall. As a student, I had had prejudices of my own, but they had more to do with the fact that the football budget was larger than that of the library and all women's sports put together than with perceived abilities of the athletes. Similarly, although I believed it was a function of the system's skewed values that football players weren't *expected* to study, the traditional brawn-or-brains dichotomy was alien to me—too many of my own friends were athletes.

I had the bookworm's conviction that everyone in the world

loved to read, whether they knew it or not—that it was simply a question of exposure—and I took the tutorial job with few preconceptions, let alone apprehensions, about what it might entail. It was an interesting proposition. I was a scholar-athlete, of sorts, about to embark upon an athletic venture for which I was ill equipped; I was to tutor athlete-scholars, of sorts, freshmen about to embark upon a momentous four-year undertaking for which they too, as I would discover, were not remotely prepared.

A visitor to Florida State's Doak Campbell Stadium today will encounter a redbrick amphitheater with a seating capacity of seventy-two thousand—incredibly, it is believed to be the largest masonry-brick project in the United States. Whole neighborhoods have been destabilized, tracts of land guzzled, and traffic patterns affected in the interest of this gargantuan facility and its constellation of associated outbuildings and acres of tarmac parking lots. A seven-story building to house a food court and gift shop is scheduled to be built behind the south end zone, and to the east a four-story addition will soon house the registrar, comptroller, financial and administration offices; in other words, under Bowden's tenure the entire nerve center of the university has been physically uprooted from its old, genteel, oak-shaded grounds and relocated wholesale in the foothills of the football stadium. With its frequent number-one pre-season ranking in the nation and its stated ten-million-dollar budget, the football team is, literally and unabashedly, what the university now revolves around.

Back in 1981, the Doak Campbell Stadium was still essentially the old, mustardy-colored ramshackle structure it had been when my family first arrived, although expanded in stages to accommodate some forty-three thousand fans. For the first tutorial session, I had been given directions to a doorway in the shadow of the stadium's underbelly and been told to proceed through the weight room to the cafeteria. There had been, then, all this time, just down the road from our house, disguised beneath the stadium's innocuous scaffolding, a kind of underground bunker, a self-contained vaguely sybaritic world. The weight room was plush with maroon carpeting and gleaming machines, unlike those seen in the health clubs or public gyms frequented by mere ordinary people but hinting at the highest body science. Later, I would learn that each machine exercised—"built up"—specific muscles; that there was even one machine designed expressly for the neck. Such knowledge may be commonplace to other people, but to me this room full of machinery devoted to the clinical, most time-effective development of the human frame was a dark revelation, as if I'd been given the key to an underground Nazi laboratory. Going through the weight room, I entered a gymnasium, around which groups of tables and chairs had been pushed back against the wall. To the right, swinging doors opened into the cafeteria, where the kitchen help were just finishing cleaning up. The dining area was immediately beyond the food counter, and when I entered this room, I found it was already full of some forty men, mostly slouched sleepily in their chairs or resting with their heads on the tables. It occurred to me that the two hours immediately following dinner, at the end of a long day of classes and grueling practice, might not be the most conducive time for a teacher to capture the attention of these particular students.

I was introduced to the study hall supervisor, a former captain of a previous squad and the dream son of every red-blooded American father. Strikingly tall and impossibly handsome in a classic, clean-cut, chiseled way, he was said to be "really smart" and preparing for med school. He was also courteous and devout in the old southern way.

"We've been studying the nervous system," he told me one evening, "all those connections, all that wiring—it's so complex you wouldn't believe it. And they want to tell us that this all evolved from some primeval soup." He snorted.

His name, somehow appropriate to the life and character that fate had scripted for him, was Scott. It was his job to take roll call and see that each student checked in with the appropriate tutor. For his obvious attributes he was respected and envied by the other players, and the gold watch and ring and other costly accoutrements that he so casually wore were admired ungrudgingly, as if all this were merely his due. It was assumed that all females would fall instant prey to his charms, and throughout the first weeks I was scrutinized closely by the roomful of players for telltale signs that I had succumbed.

"Beam me up, Scottie," a chorus of falsetto voices would wail every evening as I took my place, blushing, at his supervisory table. After roll call, I would retreat, in relief, with my charges to our class space. The specific job for which I had been hired was to tutor remedial English to a group of eight players; it was understood that there would be others along the way who needed help, but these eight—plus a ninth player who later attached himself to the group—were the ones who would report to me for two hours every night, five days a week. "Remedial English" was not the expression of choice, and I was once sternly corrected by an administrator who heard me use it. Rather, I was doling out additional English, intensive English, supplementary English, none of which, however, obscured the very basic fact that the players had been tested and found to have up to sixth-grade reading-level proficiency. Similarly, the players were not black, they were "minorities."

My group had been given a special room off the cafeteria in which to meet. There was one long table and a lot of chairs, and the room itself conjured up long strategizing sessions, jowly coaches tilting back in their chairs, diagrams on the blackboard, charts upon the table. My first impression of the players themselves, who filed into the room and took their places, all ranged along the same side of the table with their workbooks laid carefully before them, was that they seemed very young; very big, but very young. There were exchanged looks, some smirks, exaggerated expressions of interest and attention while I talked. I expounded my mission—to help them learn the grammar presented in their workbooks and to work on frequent short written essays.

"Essays!?" It was Lenny Chavers who abruptly broke the spell. Looking worriedly to the right and to the left, soliciting the support of the others, he turned to me with the grave concern of one who wants to correct a potentially embarrassing misapprehension.

"Didn't they tell you? We *can't* write. We ain't *got* no grammar."

All of the players in this initial small group were from Florida. In the eventual essays that were in fact written, one caught glimpses of their homes: Belle Glade, distinguished for its incomparable cuisine, matchless warmth and hospitality, and natural beauty—if one were to believe Jessie Hester, who was always unashamedly homesick. Panama City, where Quent Reed's uncle had a funeral parlor. Small-town Milton, where Greg Allen's mother had raised her four boys alone. A shadowy area of Tallahassee itself, of which I had never known, but where John Feagin had grown up.

The names of the players, although previously unknown to me, were familiar to many Tallahasseeans, and I found that with my new job I had suddenly become interesting to a whole new circle of people. "You know Greg Allen? Who set all those records? What's he like? Is he as shy as they say?"; "Lenny Chavers—you know, he was a wrestler before he came to Florida State"; "Coach Bowden recruited Billy when he was in England—or maybe it was Germany. He was playing in the service." I was always amazed at how much the average season-ticket holder or Tallahassee *Democrat* reader knew about the players' lives, hometowns, former achievements, along with various anecdotal information, and from these reactions I came to appreciate the fact that I now occupied privileged space. Within our classes, however, football per se was rarely discussed—coaches were, and other players, but I can never remember a game being brought up, and only rarely a practice. I had the impression that football was just a job that the players did, dispassionately, obediently, in fulfillment of their scholarship contracts. No one ever bragged about his accomplishments—he wouldn't have survived his teammates' ridicule if he did—and I never even knew what position many of them played, not that terms like "noseguard," "defensive back," and "tight end" would have meant anything to me. I had still never been to a football game.

The greatest challenge of my job was to find the right level at which to pitch the classes. Manifestly, all the students were bright, witty, and imaginative. On the other hand, many were unaware of the very fundamentals of the English language, such as, for instance, the fact that there existed something called the past tense.

"You're kidding," said Lenny when I dropped this bombshell. "I never heard that." This was true; in southern English one rarely does, the *-ed* at verb's end usually being swallowed. They listened carefully while I spoke some sentences.

"I can hear it when you talk," said Greg Allen cautiously. He meant with the English accent. But how to undo a lifetime of using what an old-fashioned grammar book might have termed "the imperfect more vivid"—"I be holding him back, telling him not to do it"; "I be running just as hard as I could"?

On top of all this was the mind-numbing fact that grammar was not an end sought for itself; that all the workbook exercises that would be so painstakingly completed were only tools to be used in the larger and more daunting task of writing and speaking.

"We ain't *got* no grammar." This had been said in much the same way that someone might declare that he had a physical handicap: "I can't play ball—I ain't *got* no hand." The proposition that these skills could be acquired, learned, was accepted with polite skepticism as a kind of high-flown abstraction, the blunt reality of the lack, of the "no grammar," neutralizing such idealism.

"How long would it take you to read a book this big?" Jessie Hester once asked me of a personal book I'd brought along to class. After a moment's hesitation, I doubled the time and, lying, replied that it would take two weeks.

"Two weeks? *Two* weeks?" Jessie's laughter showed how preposterous this was. "Caroline, I could read this book every day of my life and I would not be through in two years." He shook his head. "You gonna die of smartness. One day it's gonna come trickling out your ears."

For the first few weeks, the essay assignments I had given yielded only blank papers from half the class. I was exasperated, until I realized that this was a face-saving tactic; it was better not to try and to get a clean zero than to be perceived as making an effort and still receive an F—a strategy similar to my own fatally noncompetitive athletic competitiveness. I learned that if I graded the paper in pencil while the student was actually watching me, the results were less traumatic than if I handed it back ablaze with red lines and Xs. By the end of the semester, enough communal confidence had been gained that a player would allow, or not forbid, others to watch his paper being graded. Sprawled across the table, they would laugh or wince as each mark was made.

"There go the railroad tracks. Caroline just drew the tracks across that sentence."

It is difficult to appreciate how radical an adjustment had to be made by many of these players to all the elements of collegiate life. There was Tallahassee itself, to begin with. Many players, black and white, came from the country. One athlete (in this case, not a football but a basketball player with whom I briefly worked) recalled his first impressions of this big city, with its daunting skyscrapers and high-rise buildings—although the tallest building in the whole city at that time was our round, seven-story Holiday Inn. On the other hand, the vast, sprawling, ever greedily extending campus was genuinely intimidating to negotiate, catering by that time to more than twenty-two thousand students—approaching half the population of Tallahassee itself when my family had first arrived. There were the football apartments, which, impersonal and bluntly functional as they might be, were considered high class by some of the players—only two people, after all, shared each one. One of the members of the Extra Point Club, a booster organization which "adopted" players to help make them feel at home, described to me how one player could never be persuaded to use a bed; he had always had to sleep on the floor at home.

The players' scholarships depended upon their maintaining an acceptable grade-point average, "acceptable" in this case being defined as a 2.0, or low-C average. Anyone who fell below this was put on probation and was henceforth required to go to the evening study hall sessions beneath the stadium. A player on probation who failed to pull his grades up to the acceptable level was faced with only a few practical options: he could enroll at a junior college—a favorite, because of its proximity to F.S.U., being the Tallahassee Community College, or T.C.C.—and attempt to obtain an A.A. diploma, after which his return to Florida State could be reconsidered. In practice, this was an option that was rarely successfully taken, the logistics of enrollment, of finding an apartment, a job (there was no scholarship aid here), even a car to commute, being beyond most who attempted it. The only other constructive option was to hope to obtain a scholarship at another, lesser school. Players given this kind of second scholarship chance were generally those who were the most athletically talented of the "dropouts" and who therefore had their eyes fixed most keenly on a shot at the pros. Otherwise, there was little to be done except return home and start looking for a job. This was considered, in football parlance, to be a "downfall."

Generally, the battery of tutors employed by the athletic department was there to help the players (and less frequently other athletes) in work relating specifically to the courses they were taking. We had no association with the academic departments, which is to say that the grades that we awarded for trial or practice work counted for nothing toward the grade in the class itself. My tutorial work was done in conjunction with remedial instruction the players received from the writing lab run by the English department; it was they who had provided the grammar workbooks.

On one uncomfortable occasion, and one only, I was asked to approach a teacher on behalf of one of my players and essentially beg for an imminent F to be upgraded to a D. This came about because in commiserating with the threatened player and one of our supervisors, I indicated that I too had taken a course with this same professor and thought him to be very good but very tough. This personal association was seized upon, and I found myself saying, yes, all right, I would plead the player's case. While physically grounded on football territory, in the very shadow of the coliseum, this had seemed to me an entirely reasonable, proper, humane thing to do; above all, I had been moved by the efforts of the player in question, and I couldn't at that moment bear to see him further demoralized. This sympathetic state, however, was eroded by degrees as I made my way across the campus to the Williams Building, up the stairs into the English department, and finally into the teacher's office. I delivered my message without conviction, by now feeling very foolish. I stressed only that the player was diligent and hardworking and would profit by another chance, that he needed more time than others, and so on and on. It was a shame-making business, particularly so as I was successful.

How did I feel about compromising my own academic standards? With what mixed feelings did I participate in this desperate educational ploy? The truth is that I had no mixed feelings whatsoever. With regard to things educational, I have been called an elitist, in reference to the fact that I don't believe that higher education is for everyone. I have never confused academic ability with intelligence and have never understood, therefore, why people of manifest intelligence but no strictly academic skills should have to suffer four years (actually, closer to six years these days) laboring through a system in which they have no interest whatsoever for the sole purpose of being suitably "certified" in the eyes of society by an undergraduate degree. What is learned in these institutions is, in any case, in great part only what should have been taught in high school.

As far as I was concerned, then, there were many people at Florida State, as elsewhere, who I did not think should be where they were; and in view of the fact that their bids were accepted with straight-faced seriousness, I didn't see why a handful of athletes should not be afforded the same fictitious courtesy. True, some of the players had been tested at sixth-grade reading level, and in one or two cases even lower; today, the high school competency examination, which is given in the state of Florida to all eleventh-grade students (and which a student must pass to continue on to graduation) is pitched in eighth-grade language, the tacit understanding being that this is the level that most sev enteen-year-olds will have attained. Sixth grade, eighth grade— at this low level, what meaningful standards are really being upheld?

My own high school experience had revealed to me that it is not only athletes who stumble out of this system cheated of an education. The high school I attended from grades seven through eleven was reputedly one of the two best in the city. What we did not learn was geography, history apart from the Civil War, or English grammar. The school had good English teachers, but as it was the students who generally decided the English curriculum by vote, an unpopular subject like grammar was always avoided. We had one reading class in which we read what we wanted and were awarded points for each book. For example, I was awarded seven points for the *Iliad*, the same amount that John Biggert was given for a one-hundred-page novel about playing baseball, the justification being that I liked to read, while he did not. By the time my sister arrived in the school, four years later, books had been dispensed with and students read instead "scenarios" written by authors unknown, addressing what was felt to be the students' needs; I vividly remember the horror in our house when Joanna described how she had been made to "interact" with one such scenario pertaining to teen pregnancy.

By choice, I took Latin, taught by the redoubtable Miss Carter, and through her instruction learned obliquely some of the elements of English grammar. The math department was good, but here again it was possible to slide by, as I did, with nothing beyond Algebra II. For one semester of one year, we had an art class, in which our Scottish instructor valiantly tried to instill in us an appreciation of the old masterpieces, but after Wanda Sorrell and Sally Manners complained that we were being shown dirty pictures of naked people, that was soon put a stop to.

We did have driver's education, however, and the required class in Americanism versus Communism, and we did have thorough home economics training (also required), for both boys and girls. This class was taught by a recent graduate of Florida State, who on the first day she met with us said she wanted to "tell you a little about myself," including her fleeting aspiration to major in English at college.

"But whayn they tawld me we'd hayv to rhu-eed *Shaykspeare*? Ah sayd 'Forgit it.' "

On the two occasions my mother took jobs abroad, my sister and I essentially stopped going to school; nonetheless, when we returned to Tallahassee we had no trouble picking up where we had left off—nothing had happened in our absence. Additionally, both of us eventually graduated a year early from high school, so three full years of school had been missed with no perceptible disadvantage.

After high school, I attended Florida State, and it was here, in my freshman year, that I received with some shock the news from a kindly, old-fashioned English professor that my essays were grammatically garbled. Patiently, he went over test papers with me, explaining terms that I had only heard before in Latin, and it was thus at this late stage of the game that I discovered how abysmally ill prepared I had been. Had it not been for my own passion for reading, which I pursued to the exclusion of virtually all else, and a gift for academics that was greatly aided by our years abroad and by the fact that my family routinely and avidly discussed subjects of interest at home, I would have left high school defenseless.

In view of this personal experience, then, it struck me that the tut-tutting over the undereducated collegiate athletes was hypo-critical—the pretense being that they represented some radical deviance from their well-schooled peers. My attitude as a tutor, then, was that if the system saw fit knowingly to release ill-equipped young men and women into the world, it was catch as catch can. If some of these kids won a second chance by gaining admittance, through whatever means, to a college, then more power to them. I was therefore wholeheartedly and uncynically committed to my duties.

By the end of the first semester, the workbooks had been com-pleted, and I began working with my grammar group and some new players on the more advanced reading class. We moved out from our small room into the big gymnasium, which affected the dynamics of the tutorial sessions. Now, interested passersby—players between tutorials, players who had to be in study hall be-cause they were on probation but who were not working with any one tutor in particular—gravitated over to us, sometimes sit-ting on the outskirts of the group, sometimes listening in on the discussions. It became much harder to maintain strict control, and I settled for a compromise, seeking to work with only indi-viduals or small groups at any given moment, leaving the others more or less to their own devices as long as they stayed in their places and did not distract those of us who were working.

There is no better way to learn a subject than by teaching it to the unconverted. The announcement that we would be reading a great masterpiece of Shakespeare, for example, was not received with a glow of anticipatory excitement. Before we could think of plunging into the actual work of literature, some advance advertising had to be done on my part to sell it, and this often entailed some real soul-searching as to why it was being prescribed. *Othello*, despite the difficulties presented by its diction, was not a hard sell, principally because the play was perceived as being exclusively about an interracial "relationship," my attempts to distinguish between "the Moor of Venice" and an African African, so to speak, having been ignored.

"So she likes him," said Allen Dale Campbell, who had no official connection whatsoever with our group but had just stopped by. "Now, see, there's this white girl in my class. Now, we've been out a couple of times, but it's like people look at us funny. I told her we can't let other people stop us from doing what we want, but . . ."

"I mean, I can understand why he would get involved with her, and stuff like that, I mean what with her daddy being the prince and everything like that, and she being beautiful and everything, but what did she see in him? I mean," said Orson, swigging on the Coke mug he always carried, "it seems like it's a lot of unnecessary trouble."

For once, I appeared to have everyone's attention, and I rose to the occasion, or so I thought, explaining that from Desdemona's point of view, Othello must have been a highly glamorous figure, a man who had been out in the world and brought the world to her in her protected palace bower through the tales of his adventures.

"She says, 'I saw Othello's visage in his mind.' She means, that what she saw, *all* she saw, was what was *inside* him, his mind, the thoughts, the memories in his head."

Orson chortled. "I very much doubt that's all she saw," he said.

Isaac Bashevis Singer's "Gimpel the Fool" was greeted less sympathetically. The story's hero is an ostensibly simple man whose fellow villagers regard him as an idiot, because he allows everyone to take advantage of him. The moral point is, of course, that the "Fool's" serenity and lack of bitterness derive from his higher sensibilities, his knowledge that everything on earth is only transitory and meaningless . . . the eyes turned on me as I lectured were pitying more than contemptuous, and my voice trailed off.

"Are you saying he *knows* his wife is cheating?" John Feagin asked, his eyes narrowed.

I nodded yes.

"Caroline," said John with the patient voice of a teacher, "the man's a fool."

In November of 1982, I learned that I had obtained a job teaching at a university in central East Africa. As part of my leave-taking preparations, I had to take some grade books over to the university's writing center, where most of my students still were studying. The lady in charge introduced herself and then said, "So you're Caroline. I hear the players talk about you all the time. Honey, do you know you are probably the first smart person they have ever known who *likes* them?"

On my return from Africa, I moved away from Tallahassee, but continued to visit once or twice a year. I often wondered what each of the players I'd taught in that first remedial group had gone on to do, and on my visits home I made inquiries about them. I learned that some had graduated, but that most had not. A few had made it to the pros, and their careers at least could be tracked in the sports pages of major newspapers, but the fates of the others were less easy to determine. Only once did I actually run into one of my former charges: one summer day, I went down to the F.S.U. running track, where I bumped into Lenny Chavers and a friend.

"We're just watching that dog run off with that man's shoes," said Lenny after greeting me, his eyes fixed delightedly on a high-spirited black-and-white mongrel that could be seen in the distance, romping away from the track with something large in its mouth. Other than this encounter, however, all I came up with on casual inquiry were a handful of vague and, as it turned out, largely unsubstantiated rumors regarding the other players.

Along the way, I also discovered that by merely saying I had once tutored Florida State football players in English, I could effectively put a stop to most conversations. And whenever I brought this subject up—which I increasingly did as F.S.U.'s national ranking rose—I found that other people, people who had never met the players, were also interested in knowing what each had gone on to do. The young men in my group had been eighteen-year-old freshmen in 1981; now they would be men in their early thirties, probably with families of their own—a lifetime away from college athletics. How had they fared? Were they well? Were they happy? How, I wondered, had they come to regard their experience as athlete-scholars; was it something they would wish on their own sons and daughters? There were a number of loose ends that I wanted to see tied, and eventually I decided to make a "project" of my interest, and a determined effort to find each and every one of the old group.

Armed with information from back files of the F.S.U. football office (which gave me its complete cooperation), I began trying to trace relatives through old phone numbers and addresses. Curiously, most telephone numbers were unlisted, so this most direct means of contact quickly ran into a dead end. But eventually through relatives, friends of relatives, boosters, rumors, and other assorted means I was able to find and meet with all but one of the study group.

It was not easy for me to embark upon this project. I had not spoken with any of these men for more than a decade, and there was a chance that the voices I eventually met at the other end of the phone would be strangers to me; nor, the English-lab teacher's words notwithstanding, was I confident that all the players would remember who I was. I dreaded a cool response, the discovery that our former rapport could not exist outside the classroom. As it turned out, these fears were groundless. My request to each individual to come to his home and conduct a taped interview was in all cases greeted with graciousness and warmth.

Each of the chapters that follow is devoted to one particular player. In the case of all but two (where it will be obvious that circumstances did not permit), the interviews were taped and the majority of the text that appears represents as close to a verbatim transcript of the interviews as was possible (the nontaped interviews were written from extensive notes taken on the spot). The text is nonetheless edited, in that repetitious or extraneous material unrelated to the main concerns of the interview has been cut, as have some verbal tics (that is, not every instance of "like," "you know," or other fillers of this kind has been recorded). Some rearrangement of the text was also made in the interest of coherency, but great care was taken to ensure that no stray single sentence or thought would be moved or taken out of its context. Punctuation and paragraph breaks were made with a view of duplicating as closely as possible the natural rhythm of the speaker's speech.

Above all, I resisted the temptation to tidy up another person's words; I had come to know these men in the course of correcting their language, and I felt strongly that there was now a poetic justice in letting each have his own say, in his own way.

Years ago, I had caught glimpses of the lives of my former students through their comments in class and especially through the essays they had written. People who knew me were often bemused by what they considered to be my unlikely affinity for these players. For my own part, it was only recently that I came to realize that the reason these life stories were so compelling to me was largely because at some unconscious level I have always recognized in them, through a glass darkly, elements of my own.

GREG

Greg Allen was the rising star of the team. In October of 1981, Ricky Williams, the starting running back of choice, was injured, and freshman Allen was substituted for the upcoming game against L.S.U. Although Greg had clocked the second-fastest sprint time on the squad (4.6 seconds for 40 yards), no one was prepared for his breakaway performance that night, when he ran for 202 yards on twenty-one carries, breaking F.S.U.'s single-game rushing record. Starting the following week against Western Carolina, he racked up 322 yards on thirty-two carries, a feat that was hailed by the local press as "perhaps the greatest individual performance in Florida State history at home." He was to finish the season with the N.C.A.A. rushing record for freshmen and ranked as one of the top two players of his position in the Southeast. As the records fell, the national sports press descended on Tallahassee for television and published interviews with the sensational running back from Milton, Florida; in 1981, one must remember, Florida State had been ranked only ninth in Associated Press preseason polls, and attention of this kind was not run of the mill.

Greg was an attractive man, with an approachable, kind face and sleepy eyes. He was highly popular, mixing and laughing easily with everyone, and yet one also sensed a constraint that checked complete spontaneity, as if some unseen authority were monitoring his thoughts and actions. Greg was under six feet tall, but his physique was a matter of comment even among the other players; when, years later, I visited the other members of the group, a common question was "Does Greg still look good?"

In addition to playing football, Greg was on the track team, his speciality being the triple jump. One night at study hall, he nonchalantly executed a standing back flip (which was instantly capped, however, by Jessie Hester's flashier running back handspring, followed by a sailing layout back flip). In general, however, Greg's extreme diffidence kept him from doing anything that might draw attention to himself off the field. This constitutional modesty would occasionally manifest itself in unexpected ways.

"Why aren't you with the others, with the biology tutor?" I asked one night, seeing him sitting on his own in a corner, reading. "They're reviewing for a test."

"They be over there talking dirty," he said in his soft voice; and from this I gathered that they were discussing the reproduction of the species.

The ruling figure of Greg's life was his mother; one could virtually see her presence standing watchfully behind him with an upraised admonitory finger—it was she, there could be no doubt, who had instilled in him that internal, self-corrective restraint that now guided his every action.

"Greg's apartment was always packed with people after a game," a friend of his from Florida State days told me. "He had a big supportive family, and there were always cousins and nephews and uncles around. Greg would greet them, but he would watch the door, and when she came in, he went straight to Mom. She was a very special lady."

Apart from his remarkable athletic talents, Greg's most striking attribute, even had he not possessed the star status that he did on the team, was his shyness. Twelve years later, when I was inquiring as to his whereabouts, people would say with wonder,

"I never could believe that Greg Allen majored in *communica-tions*??!"

At the end of one session during the first week we met for tutorials, Greg had hung back after class, waiting for everyone else to leave the room.

"Do I speak country?" he asked me softly, when the coast was clear, his books stacked with conscientious neatness under his arm. I sensed then, as I often would later, the weight of hidden, wearying responsibilities that would always beset his life; if the reply he received was in the affirmative—"Yes, you do speak 'country' "—it would be absorbed by him as a personal, almost moral failing that it would ever be his duty to correct. It occurred to me that he must have endured many unintentional rebukes, and that one had to tread carefully with him.

In fact, Greg's way of speech and, above all, his voice were others of his outstanding attributes: slow, warm, yet with a deep, masculine timbre uncharacteristic of the regional drawl; a voice—the cliché is unavoidable—that flowed like dark southern molasses. His speech—*when* he spoke—was modulated by an instinctive cadence.

"You can't use 'like' in this sense," I once told him, correcting an essay he had written. " '*Like*, we were doing this,' '*Like*, we thought.' It's commonly spoken, but it sounds sloppy and it's not correct—you can't get away with it in a written composition. You can say 'for example,' " I concluded, but this sounded hard and wrong even as I said it.

Greg shook his head.

" 'Although'? 'On the one hand'?" We reached an impasse, and I momentarily had to leave the issue to one side. But some minutes later, Greg spoke up from his corner of the room. " 'Whereas,' " he said quietly.

My impression of Greg's schoolwork was that he was in over his head, but that he was diligent, conscientious, and trying very hard; at least, he was never on academic probation. He could always be counted on to do what he was told, as was most poignantly illustrated by an incident in a P.E. class he was then taking. He and his classmates were told to line up, four at a time, at the deep end of the old Montgomery Gym indoor swimming pool, jump in, and swim a lap. Greg's turn came; he jumped— and plummeted like a stone to the bottom. He wouldn't have dreamed of calling attention to himself by admitting he couldn't swim.

Unlike some other athletes who were clearly destined for the pros, Greg wanted his degree, and I believed that in the long run—and it might well take a long run—he would get it. Only once, to my knowledge, did he commit an academic "indiscretion," turning up at study hall one night with an essay for his Family Living class due the next day, which had obviously been written by someone else—as I recall, it was even in the other person's handwriting. I didn't bother to read it, but handed it back with the suggestion that he get the person who wrote it for him to correct it. He stood in complete silence for several minutes, incapable of attempting to put up a defense, and eventually he just picked up his books and left.

"Greg says you're mad at him," John Feagin told me later in the session. He had evidently passed Greg on his way out. "He told me, 'Caroline knew that I didn't write that paper, and now she's mad at me.' I told him it weren't just him; you been mad at me, and Lenny too."

This was on a Thursday evening. That weekend there was an away game, and everyone was packed up and gone by Friday afternoon, but Sunday evening they were back at study hall. Greg was absent from roll call, but came running in some minutes later, breathing hard, and half threw a paper on the table where I sat.

"I didn't turn the other one in," he said. "I swear to God I wrote the whole thing," he continued, watching me pick up what he had put before me, and I realized from the emotion in his voice that his breathlessness was not due solely to the fact that he had run over from the apartments. "I took it up to L.S.U. and wrote it over the weekend."

It was at L.S.U., one should remember, that Greg had first revealed himself to be a potential star. He left me alone to read the essay, which I found painful to think would soon be submitted the next day for a grade.

"My mother is two parents to four boys," he had written. "It was hard for her to bring us up. We would get dinner for her and run her bath water—we tried to do everything we could to help her. It hurt us to see how tired she was.

"She no longer sends notes to me like she did at first. She knows that I will do the right thing. She wrote, 'I brought you up right.' I carry that note with me always."

The first thing that everyone said to me when recently I started making inquiries about Greg was "You know his mother died?" She had passed away, appropriately, in church, but had lived long enough to see her son inducted into the Florida State Hall of Fame, just two months earlier.

"A sweet, special lady," I was told, again and again. "Shy and humble, and thankful for Greg's abilities."

After F.S.U., Greg had played briefly with the Cleveland Browns and had then returned to Milton and worked construction with one of his brothers for a while, before eventually landing a job in a bank in Pensacola. Most people I spoke with, however, seemed to think he was back in Milton these days. When I got his address and telephone number I saw that he was not only back in Milton but back in his mother's house.

"Yeeeaahhhh, I remember you," said Greg when I telephoned. "Over the years, I thought of you. I used to look for your name in the paper. You talked proper." His own voice was as languidly, darkly sonorous as ever. "I married my high school sweetheart; we have two sons; and we had one daughter on the outside. Yeah, I ended up back here. I was living in Pensacola— I had a town house there—but I gave that up and came here and took over my mother's mortgage."

*   *   *

Few of the players had really talked about their hometown or about their homes in any way that had left a vivid impression of where they came from. But Greg had often referred to Milton, even to the road he lived on—Persimmon Hollow Way—and I found that when I set out to Milton, I did so with the same kind of anticipation I would bring in going to a historic landmark. Milton is situated in the extreme northwest of the Florida panhandle, only miles northeast of Pensacola. Historically, it was an important sawmill town and port, situated on the Blackwater River, an artery of the Blackwater and Escambia Bays. The once-bustling town suffered in the Civil War; as one unforgiving local historian has written, "The importance of this area's industrial capacity made it prey to destructive raids by Yankee troops." Quiet, partially forgotten, taking second place to nearby Pensacola, Milton is nonetheless a pretty town, with old brick houses, built when there had been local brickyards, and a well-kept historical district.

Greg's mother had lived outside of Milton itself, off Highway 90, the main conduit into town. Persimmon Hollow Way was, as I had always imagined it, a narrow, peaceful road, somewhat crowded in this summer season with tall grass, and flanked by rows of bungalows and some trailers in modest but comfortable gardens.

Greg met me at his house, a smart brick bungalow on a corner plot, with a pickup truck parked outside. He had apparently not aged at all, and it occurred to me, as I looked at him with a kind of wonderment, that time must just pass more slowly in Milton. His shyness was still detectable, but so too was the new confidence of being in his element: he was meeting me on home ground.

His house was furnished with great simplicity: the small living room was filled by a matching chair and sofa, an old upright piano, and a coffee table on which were set two books—the Holy Bible and the wedding album of Greg and Mary Allen. Three pictures adorned the walls, all hung over the piano, and all photos of F.S.U.'s number 26 in action.

Greg settled down, settled deeply, into what was clearly *his* place, the chair that immediately faced the door; the hours in which he had sat just here throughout his life, watching life pass beyond the screen wire door, were, I imagined, incalculable. It struck me now, seeing him command his small view, that although he had not appreciably aged he had become a patriarch. Unquestionably, Greg was at home—home, home, home. Home in Milton, home in his mother's house.

Although he was considerably more at ease, his eyes had their old look of careful watchfulness. By way of confession, and to get it over with, he told me he had never finished his degree.

"I took some correspondence courses in Cleveland, but, you know, with practice, there wasn't much time to study. At Florida State, what with summer school and the regular terms, I managed to get it down to three classes a term. But I changed over to a communication major the year before, and then I got into the workforce, and that kind of put drags on things. Then before that, I was moving and carrying—I was a professional: I stayed in there about two years.

"People pretty much know—you know—who's gonna go to the pros and who's not. It's not much difference between the players, it's just the publicity each one gets. Let's take—you probably know Dennis McKinnon. He play with Chicago. Well, his senior year, they hardly ever played him, and they was playing Jessie Hester, and I think—let's see—I think Jessie must have been a sophomore. Well, he wasn't getting any of the publicity that Jessie was getting, being a rookie coming in and doing good. But he did get drafted to Chicago, Des McKinnon did, and did well for them—even won the championship that the Bears won. So it wasn't much of a difference between the two athletes—they both was receivers and they can catch good—but Jessie was in that limelight and McKinnon was getting ready to go on, to graduate, so they promote their incoming and kinda fade out on their outgoing. It's the same way with me and Ricky Williams, that was the running back. They came out with me, and Ricky started to gradually fade away as he got closer to graduation; and then after

I got hurt, I wasn't playin' anymore, and I started gradually just fading away, and Sandy Smith started coming in.

"My senior year at Florida State, I had tore up my knee. It was about the eighth game of the season, so I had about three more games before the draft, and I tore up some cartilage; but I still got drafted in the second round, played around about two years for Cleveland. I wouldn't have wanted to stay long—just long enough to advance, you know, to get a head start, save me up some money and that's just basically it. Because from seventh grade to college, I mean that's a lot of miles—that's a lot of miles in running on those legs.

"After I left Cleveland, I got drafted to Tampa Bay." He gave a deep sigh. "Not drafted, but I went to Tampa Bay; I signed a contract with Tampa Bay. And after that contract, I went to Indianapolis and I was there, and I played through spring ball and then I just kinda, you know, just withdrew. Because I knew my knee wasn't going to get any better. What happened is the fluid would build up on it, and it would be so *tight*, you know, so I just said there's no use in me crippling myself for life, so I kinda pulled out and then I did get released with Indianapolis so they kinda made up my mind for me. It was hard to let go; it was hard to let go. But finally I did, and now that I'm thirty I think about this. It would be four years ago that I made up my mind to stop trying. That's about it. I can still feel the injuries, you know; when I get up in the morning, it's a little bit stiff and, like, in my elbow here, I can feel probably the cartilage wearing out or something. I do have a separated shoulder." He sighed again.

"The pros was not a lifestyle I would have wanted for long. I wouldn't have wanted it for long. I could take it for—if I would had played, I would had played about five years—that's it. You get to be a certain age, you just—especially being a running back, being the person that gets hit all the time. I think I could have took about five years of it. Do I miss the limelight? In a sense, in a sense I do; but then, doing the time, I would hide, you know, take a different route to avoid the press and stuff like that, and sign autographs.

"I was recruited to Florida State in my senior year—they couldn't talk to you until you become a senior, so that's when I started getting letters and stuff like that, and some phone calls; it was something else. At first it was exciting, seeing mail come from different colleges, then it started getting—they call you on the phone, and say 'We want you to come up and visit us,' and then you got to know where they are—you take some of their cards; I kinda got tired of it.

"I didn't know right off that I was going to Florida State. Not really. You know, like, some kids from the ninth grade on up, they say 'Florida State is where we want to go.' I hadn't made up my mind. I had been to Tallahassee before coming to Florida State; I had a cousin went to law school there, so I spent some time there. It wasn't that much of a change—it wasn't like going to Miami or anything like that. I was familiar with the area—but I didn't know until I started getting mail and, you know, people was interested and coming to town; that's when I started realizing, I'm gonna go to college. My mother always told us that she wanted us to go to college, but as far as using football skills to get there, I was playing the game for fun—it was just a thing that the males did in the family—everybody played football if you were a male. But when I started to catch on to it and, like I said, people started coming and stuff, people started saying you can go on scholarship."

And what, I asked, about Florida State? How had that turned out? "Florida State?" He sighed again, measuring his words. "I think it was an experience . . . I did get something out of it. Well, actually, when I went to Florida State, I really learned how to study and to, you know, do the basic things of education. In high school I just kind of, you know, flagged it, just did enough to get by, and I think a lot of that has to do with—that I had a single parent, and she was working and there just wasn't nobody there to *push*, push, you know. She just didn't physically have the time to push.

"You know, it's not that we didn't *know* anything, it's that we was never taught—like English, for instance. In high school, we read just for lessons, to do my lessons. Probably, when I was younger I had to read out in class or something, but as far as just sitting down and reading—well, how about some of those bedtime stories, those little short books and stuff like that? Yes, I've done that. But somewhere in, probably elementary and through middle school, they kinda give that up. I didn't see any preparation in high school, that they was making it a point that I take certain classes to prepare me for college. I imagine that if I was an A-B Honor Roll student then, you know, I think people maybe would have taken an interest, maybe said 'You need to take this or that'—that type of thing, paid more attention.

"We did English out of the workbook, you know, you do those little exercises and stuff like that, but we was not really *taught* English. You know what I mean? Then I get to Florida State and had to write a paper; a *term* paper." He shook his head and laughed. "I was expecting it be hard. I was expecting that. But as far as knowing how hard, or what I had to do—no. I didn't have any idea.

"For my first English assignment, I had to think 'How to do this.' " He laughed again in disbelief. "What I'm gonna write about, you know? First of all, I had to just determine what it was, you know, what was a paper? What was it involved? How do I start this thing? What do I talk about? How do I break my subjects up and, you know, just that—just trying to identify what it was.

"I took some theater classes; that's about the only ones I enjoyed. Some improv. That was relaxed. The other stuff—history and English and math—whew! I thought I liked math, but—I was real tense. It was a bit frustrating. It wasn't the time to play catch-up. It wasn't. It was like they just throw you in there and expect you to do it. Even if you didn't know how to do it, you had to pretend you know how to.

"Their expectations, I think, it was just as realistic as you want it to be. Take Rosie Snipes. Skipped class, never go to class, you know that type of thing. They had to make him go to study hall, and stuff like that. But for me, you know—well, I skipped some classes, but I made it my part to be there too, to learn, and I focused on that's why I was there, to get an education, because they gonna get what they want from you, so you gotta get what you want. If I needed a tutor I said, 'Hey, I need a tutor for this subject,' and they give it to me. So I think it was just as realistic as you want it to be.

"The only thing—you know what?" He looked at me cautiously. "Only thing I would miss is that I was a reader. A reader. If I could just be a bookworm, or something, and just read and read—you know. Math? Just give me a little bit of math, just to figure out the basic problems. But reading, I think I could have gone"—he paused—"beyond. That's all. What I find about reading now, and I guess it comes from not doing it so much, is that, for me, I have to *concentrate*," he said, weighing the words. "I have to *focus* and get into the story, you know? It's kinda hard for me to sit here and read, focus and get that understanding, all together. It's seeing if you can relate yourself to it. I've been doing some reading, you know, like at night, I've been making myself read. I tote a book around." He laughed, briefly turning his face away. "I tote a book—it's in the truck right now. It's by Stephen King. *The Stand*. So that's what I'm doing, you know, I just tote a book and just make myself read.

"It was just—you know what? I think in high school it would have been too late. I think that—what's the age they learn the most? Around twelve, ten to twelve. So you have to start early, you have to start early, getting the basic reading and mathematics and then as it goes, after you learn to read and, you know, read good and stuff, it goes on up; you start gradually going up. The only teacher I remember in high school is Mr. Lynn. His folks was in the education system too. And the reason why I remember, it was math, and I liked math a whole lot, and we always be competitive against each other within the class. You know, I made A's and B's in math; that's the only class that I can remember that doing good was rewarded, you know that type of thing. As far as elementary, I couldn't even tell you the teachers who—pushed, who emphasized education—really."

The screen door opened and two little boys of about eight and twelve walked in, tall and long limbed and simmering with barely contained mirth.

"This here is Greg Junior and Emery," said Greg. "Caroline here is the lady I said used to be my teacher." Greg Junior had heard that I had lived in Africa and wanted to know about the bears and tigers over there. There were no bears and tigers, but I told him instead about the gorillas I had seen in the mountains of Rwanda, bigger than him, with hands nearly as big as his head and facial expressions that were just like those of human beings. Greg Junior stood stock still, unblinking, and later in the day appeared again, coming through the screen door with two other small boys.

"Will you tell my friends what you told me about the gorillas?"

There was lots of family around Milton. Greg's sister-in-law dropped in with her little girl of two, who stood in the middle of the room with her chubby hands clenched into little fists, looking in wide-eyed and ferocious amazement from one adult to the other.

"I hear you give hugs," said Greg to her from his easy chair. "No? Well, that's what they tell me." The phone on the wall between the living room and the kitchen behind us rang, and he leaped up to answer, knowing, I felt, who was at the other end.

"Mary? Mary who? I don't have no wife." I had the sense that this is how it must always have been in this small house, reliably always here, in the tall grass of Persimmon Hollow Way, sitting comfortably, for all his mother's toil and hardship, behind its screened door in readiness to receive whatever friend or relative might drop in. Mary Allen worked at a bank in Milton. A pretty, poised, and gregarious woman, she, I imagined, drummed up all the social occasions, got the parties going, catered to the streams of visitors that came laughing into the Allen home, while Greg sat basking in the noise and the activity, stepping in and out as his mood took him.

"Me and Mary, we've been together for fourteen years," he said fondly, in the settled tones of an old married man twice his age.

Greg's oldest brother lived in Atlanta, where he was a manager at Wal-Mart and still going to school.

"My other brother does contract work here, and the *other* does land work," Greg said, filling in the family history when everyone had gone. "Myself, I'm a manager at Albertson's. Y'all have an Albertson's supermarket in Tallahassee? I'm a night manager out in Fort Walton. Twelve to nine and four to one, on different days. I get to be here during the day, so it suits me.

"Greg Junior, I already know he's going to be athletic. But I want to hold him back—he already wants to play Little League football. I'm holding him back so he doesn't burn out. Greg used to go to the games. We had him early, you know, in high school. Emery, all he sees is just the tapes I got, of when I played. I must have watched those things a thousand times.

"What I am trying to focus on in my life is my kids' education. I figure that if I push them hard now, that later on it will be easier for them. Greg is an excellent reader; they say he'll be honor roll, and I think it partly comes from me and my wife working together and, you know, just making him do it.

"Would the high school let him slide by? You know I think, I think some teachers—yes. I think that if it was left up to them they would let them slide by. And, you know some teachers do care—I can't say every teacher's like that, but I also think that, you know, that it comes from the home first. If it's not important at home for him to get his work, then how do you expect the teacher to make him get it? So, we have to start here and let him know how important it is, and what we are expecting for him to do when he's at school. Like this summer, I have Greg read at least a chapter at night. Sometime I think I'm pushing too hard with him and I slack up some, but I think when he get older, he'll appreciate, and maybe he'll push his as hard as I did him. That's the reward I'm lookin' for, down the line.

"The schools are different. Now, I used to live out in Pensacola, and Greg Junior used to go to the elementary school in Pensacola, over in a majority white area, you know, where—very high standards to pass. I mean he was home doing homework, and me and his mother stayin' up late, you know, and he still makin' A's and B's. He liked the school. Now he moved over to Milton, to the East Side School, right down the road here, and it wasn't a challenge for him. He just go right through it. You know, he didn't have to study, he didn't have to work at it.

"Now it just goes to show—why change the system because of the . . . the—not ethnic, but economics? Maybe because it's a poor area over here—but why change the two systems? You got the same kids; I think maybe they have the same ability to learn; you got teachers that went and got the same educations, so they have the ability to teach the same thing—so why change the system from this here to this here? You gotta mind that some people are slower than others, but then you use a different technique to teach the slower. But why not just have one system, everybody works under the same system, and you stress education? You know, it's awful easy—here in Milton, they don't even—I don't think they've even, haven't even thought about it. Milton is a country town," said Greg, not without, I suspected, a twinge at his disloyalty. "So they feel that—they probably think that the system is right here. You know, think 'My kid's gettin' the best education.' Which over in Pensacola—it's like first-graders there is like second-graders here. I mean, that's how much advanced they are over there. I mean, we had homework, I'm talkin' about stuff that brought some"—he laughed—"brought some memories back, you know—you had to think awhile.

"But I think, I don't even know how you would change the system over at this point. It's just not taken serious here—the school system. If you take one of those kids that's on the street, and if you could take him back through high school, give him the proper education, and you know, maybe he'd be on the honor roll this time instead of D's and F's, do you think he would be out on the street? He wouldn't be. He would be a different person. *Totally* different. Most of them are out on the street just because it's a simple thing to do—hang out. You know, they don't have any pressure, they . . . they just there. And that's—*nowhere to go*. It's too late now.

"If Quentin Reed was an excellent student, he would have had somewhere to turn to. But if he didn't have somewhere to turn to and he go back home—here's Quentin Reed not taught how to do anything; he's back in town. He's not working—it's a downfall. I can understand, you know, why people would turn to—I never done drugs; I never even ssssmmmoked a rrreefer," he said, dragging on the words. "It was just something that I was scared I would get hooked on, or like, and do it all the time. But I can understand why somebody would turn to that. And they always have a different perspective of how *they* are going to handle it; they think that if they gonna do it this way, they won't get like this guy over here.

"If I was a principal, I would want—reading and English would be the most important thing. Because if you can read and understand what you reading, you know, if you can read, you can understand. And it's a way to communicate. You don't communicate by arithmetic, right? So, you know, with the verbal education, you can make it. That's basically what everything is. Except engineering and science and stuff like that. But if people can read and understand what they are reading, or what is being said to them, that would change a whole lot of things.

"You know, like I was tellin' my wife the other night, I said I would give anything just to be a bookworm. Just to read, read, read. And she asked me, 'Why?' And I said, you know, just to have the knowledge—just to read from the text and just have it in your head and be able to speak well and know hard words and—just have it. I can't remember if it was you or not," he said, suddenly shy, "that said you need to read more, read anything, even if it's *Playboy* magazine—whatever interests you; that stuck in my mind. That's why I remembered Caroline so well. When I saw right here by the phone 'Caroline Alexander' and this Tallahassee number—"

Encouraged, I asked boldly—as I didn't have the heart to do

in most of the interviews—if anything had stayed with him from the tutorials.

"I think it do," he said gallantly. "I can still—I can write papers; I can still remember formats.

"Goin' back. My mother got pregnant and she dropped out of school. It's from back there to now. You know, people back then—black people back then—wasn't educated, so there's so much that they—you know, I know a little bit more than my parents because I went to college, and I know why this thing's important. It's important. Then I pushed myself to get this education, because I know how important it is. My mother was a janitor, and she worked in a rest home; but I know that if she had the education, if her mother before her which had a sixth-grade education and had taught herself how to read—excellent reader! excellent!—if she would have pushed her, she would have pushed me.

"My mother, she had to play Mom and Dad. We always get these quotes from her, what her dad had taught them. She always emphasized on, 'If my dad was living . . . ,' 'If your granddad was living, you couldn't lay in this bed this late in the day,' you know? That's how she gave us a male figure. 'You need to be out doing *something*. Working in the yard; clean up this house.' There was just these things she'd tell us; 'You got to watch what you say.' You know, 'Think twice, and speak once.' Just always those little words to keep us on track. It helped.

"Every morning she called me at school. *Every* morning. Even when I got married! She still called me early in the morning. It was six a.m. Tallahassee time, and I just rolled out of the bed, and would say, 'Why are you callin' me this early?' 'I want to know you gettin' up to go to school. It's time to get up!' I miss that. It's one of those things. So I ended up living here and took over the mortgage. The other guys too, so all of us own the house, but I just . . . but I probably won't end up living here my whole natural life," he said watching my face with some attention. "I'll build a place of my own."

I said that I would find it hard to leave, and he seemed to relax.
"Yes, it is kinda hard. I kinda want to buy it from them."
It was late in the afternoon when I got up to depart, and the
light coming through the screened door and windows was soft
and low. In the doorway, I turned to ask a final question.
"Would getting your degree help you now? In life? In your
present job?"
"Yes, it would! I think it was just having that stamp of ap-
proval." He was holding the door open for me, his face expec-
tant and watchful. He knew what was coming. "I think it would
make a difference." There was a long pause.
"Will you pursue it?"
He sighed. "If I can find some time."
"It's how many courses that you lack?"
"Three."
"Three? That's all?"
"I looked into it. Actually they changed the whole system—
the requirements—but I got it approved and everything, under
the old system, and can go ahead and graduate; they added a
math to it, and I still kept two other classes to take."
"Greg, you could do it in a year."
"I know. I know. I would probably do it at the university, at
West Florida."
"One year and you would have it for the rest of your life.
You're thirty, and you would have it until you're ninety."
He laughed slowly, looking away, back into the house.
"Just do it. One course at a time; because you're up to it."
He looked back at me, all the old pain of responsibility sud-
denly in his eyes, the look of twelve years ago when he would
stand unfathomably quiet, perhaps cut to the quick, listening, affected. I knew he would turn this over and over in his mind, discuss it with Mary; and I could see the spectral admonitory finger
upraised above his head, more palpable than ever, in his
mother's house.

JOHN

It was Jessie Hester who one night gave the most memorable characterization of John Feagin: opening his eyes wide and turning his head from side to side in mock wonderment, he did a little pantomime of John arriving in South Florida with the Haitian boat people.

"Here I come, wearing my banana-leaf shoes," Jessie said, lifting his feet with exaggerated care, while the rest of the group, John included, laughed until tears filled their eyes. As usual, although the result of inspired whimsy, Jessie's skit contained just enough recognizably true-to-life details to make the image he was projecting "catch." John's skin was dark, like a Haitian's, and he was tall and lithe—he didn't carry the weight the others did, and looking at him one would not have immediately guessed that he played football.

Moreover, John did at times have the air of a man who had in fact come from somewhere else. When I spoke in class, for instance, he listened with attention so close as to imply that whatever was being said was extremely new to him. And like a person who is still learning the ropes in a foreign land, he seemed to take for granted that it was in the natural scheme of things that he should walk away from every exchange without full comprehension.

"Oh, OK," he used to say, as if to register the fact that I had done my job of imparting certain information. The second stage—figuring out the information—he seemed to assume was his private task, and rarely did he presume to tax me further by asking for explanations of what I had said, or meant to say, or meant.

In class, he was quiet, well behaved—in another age one would have said "well brought up"—and his good manners were graceful and unfailing. At the beginning of every session, it was John who would go off on his own accord to find me a chair, or who would carefully hold a door open for me when he saw that my arms were full of books. But though he was reliable and quiet, he was no goody-goody, and his flashes of humor could be sharp.

"Now why would she spend all that money, at her age, to fix her teeth?" he complained of an older supervisor, who had just got braces. "By the time her teeth are straight, she'll be dead. And why fix on her teeth, when her face look like"—he smacked a fist into his open hand—"she been hit head-on by a Mack truck?"

I felt that while John had the innate capacity to grasp whatever was being taught, somehow, somewhere along the line, the ground rules for learning, the most fundamental logical principles, had been given to him wrong, or skewed in some quaint, perhaps now-obsolete form, which he could never quite get around. A case in point was the "compare and contrast" paper, a favorite composition assignment in the basic English class that most of the athletes were taking—an exercise as unimaginative as it sounds. The only white students I dealt with, two Florida country boys whom I worked with on three or four occasions, came up with the kind of model paper (curiously identical to each other's) sought by the teacher:

COMPARE AND CONTRAST
A TELEVISION AND A RADIO

A television and a radio are both means of communication. On the one hand, both have audible aspects, and many stations. On the other hand, a television has pictures and a radio does not. . . .

John Feagin's topic was "Compare and Contrast an Apartment Building and Living in a Trailer in a Hurricane." To clarify: The features of an apartment (in any weather) were compared to living in a trailer in a hurricane. On the one hand, John's paper was clearly the more interesting and instructive; on the other, it was just left of center when it came to the topic's structural logic.

John was quietly struggling, perhaps not clear himself as to whether he was losing the battle or holding even. But I find that when I look back at those class sessions, he was always there, on time, accountable, with his work—in whatever state—conscientiously done, and ready to lend a hand to me whenever it might be required. "You-all be quiet!" he would say, "Caroline trying to talk." He was in fact, I realize now, my right-hand man.

Like me, John was from Tallahassee. He was a graduate of Leon High, at one time a first-rate school and still regarded as the best public high school in the city. John was the least difficult of the players to find years later; he was listed in the Tallahassee directory, at the same address I had for him from twelve years before.

Hunter Road, where his family lived, was a hidden oasis of almost rural peace tucked behind one of Tallahassee's major thruways. While the neighborhood as a whole seemed quiet, its streets close with greenery and blooming crepe myrtle, Hunter Road was, even in relation to these, exceptional. John's house was one of only three on the entire street, the other two being still under construction at the far end of the road. The lot adjacent to his house had been turned into a flourishing vegetable garden, and high grass and a grand live oak tree commanded the uncultivated area opposite. A short distance beyond, the road came to a quiet, leafy dead end, thus ensuring that it remain an essentially closed and private domain.

John's father, Reverend Feagin, was just leaving for work when I arrived. He was a strikingly handsome, athletic-looking man with alert, bemused, twinkling eyes. John Feagin Sr. ran his own landscaping business, in which John Junior at times helped out—a fact that put into perspective earlier reports I had had that John was "raking yards in Tallahassee."

"My father, he loooooves standing back and looking at land he's finished," John said later, and I thought that this characterized the Feagin home as a whole, which exuded the cozy, settled air of a much-tended object accustomed to being viewed with satisfaction.

John himself met me at the door. He had put on weight over the years, even developing a slight paunch, and actually looked taller than I had remembered him. Always deliberate and slow in his movements, he now seemed to move more heavily. Inside, a tower of athletic trophies—belonging to John and to his sister— presided over the kitchen cabinet.

"Yeah, I remember you," he had said when I first called. "In fact, I've often thought of you. I didn't think I'd see you again," he added ambiguously. He was as deferential as before, but I had the impression that he was looking forward to talking. His house was generous and sprawling—more like two distinct houses joined together—and we made our way through to the backmost section, paneled in dark wood, which belonged to the "children."

John's brief two years at Florida State still loomed large in his mind—or, rather, in his psyche—and the brutal abruptness of his departure in 1982 was something that even now, all these years later, he did not seem to have completely absorbed.

"It was pretty much round that same time that you left that all the ones that they say were suspended for a while, as far as gradewise, they called into this office and said 'You-all get your stuff ready and you-all got to go.' And it's like all of a sudden, quickly, we were out. It was at the end of the term. A couple of people had already known, but the office was hush-hush about it, and then they announced those they said were suspended because of grades.

"Everyone was, 'I will help you in any way I can,' and whatever and whatever, but when they brought on the list saying who all need to get out of their apartment, they didn't try to help me, as far as move my stuff, or anything. They just said 'Well—you-all gotta go. See ya.' So that really hurt me then—I didn't understand that aspect of them just saying 'Hey, we don't have nothing else to do with you at all.' All my awards, like the Gator Bowl Award, the plaque—I didn't get that; there were a lot of different awards that I was there with the team when we played them, in the Gator Bowl—that really hurt.

"It was tough for people out of town. Quent Reed, he was tough. He had to—he called someone because, like I said, he was my roommate, and he called some guy to come pick him up that lived here in Tallahassee. He took all of his stuff over to the guy's house. He stayed here for about two and a half weeks before he even told his parents. For me, to tell my parents, even that—but I knew they would understand. I loaded everything up, and came back here. I think we had about two days' notice. Not *weeks*. No weeks, no. No, no—not even a week. I had to leave before Sunday. It was like the nineteenth, and before the twenty-third you have to vacate—they give you a list, they give you a memo. You have to be out; if not, they will take your stuff out. So they more like kick you out. They don't have anything else to do with you. When you get out, that's it." (The football office's comment is that a player who has flunked out is no longer under contract with the school, and N.C.A.A. regulations prohibit the player from receiving further benefits.)

"OK, really I think what happened to me was when I broke my foot; when I broke my—you didn't know I had crutches? When I broke my foot, everything changed. It was like, I didn't know who was what. I didn't really know what was going on then; it was really some changes. I was redshirted for a year, you know, you don't play in the games or anything like that, so it was like they put you aside; they use you as a dummy. For drills or anything you involved in—you just there, to show the other guys.

"I can understand how with someone like Quent, it would

make him take the wrong path. 'Cos it crossed my mind to do something. Yeah, it did. Because I was—it was like totally different from high school. In my high school, coach Gene Cox, he was like if you got in trouble, at times, and you were one of the players, he would come to your house, talk to your parents. We had a lot of guys that did do different things, get into problems, you know, different problems in school, and he would come to your house and talk and stuff like that and things would get better. It was a point that he was making, that he was a caring coach. He wanted you to know more and go farther than just football; but those coaches up there at Florida State, they didn't care. They just, I guess, like saving some money.

"My family helped me a whooole lot. When everyone turns back on you, it's hard to bounce back. You really need someone to help you, and they're the ones that brought me out of it. And life goes on. Try it again, or whatever you like to do. They didn't push me to go back to school, and they didn't push me to try and play football again. I think more my main thing, my motivation was cut off; my self-esteem, my motivation, everything was out for grabs. So I worked with my dad; and I could see people on Saturdays going into the games; I'm not working Saturdays, and it was a kind of hurting thing.

"I chose Florida State because—well as far as a mind thing, they emphasized a lot your home, you're close around home, you know—'You don't have to leave,' and 'A lot of people around Tallahassee would push you and be behind you' and this and that, so that's really what made me think about it. I never been away from home as far as school-wise; if I'm out of town, I'm with my family. You know that counted, that influenced; I'm not saying I picked the wrong college, which I don't think I did, but I think if I would have gotten away from home, made some new friends and done different things, instead of coming out of high school—

"Leon is a great school," said John. I replied that it couldn't have been that great, or he would have been better prepared for

college. He grinned. "OK, yeah, I *was* ill prepared. I think my—
OK, going through from my ninth grade through twelfth; in my
ninth-grade year, I played football, OK, it was a great year for
me, for my playing football. My tenth-grade year, I didn't, you
know, because I quit my tenth-grade year to work with my father
to pay for a car; I got a car when I turned sixteen and it was like
a decision of football or a car, so I didn't play. And the teachers
were on me my ninth-grade year—everybody was like 'Well, are
you going to college and play football?' Then, in my tenth-grade
year, I worked, you know, I was into school and everything, but
I wasn't really into football; so they were like, 'If he's not into
football, he's not really into college.' I'm not saying all the teachers were like this, every last one of them, but the majority of
them, they didn't push me anymore.

"My ninth grade, when I was coming up breaking all the tackle
records and many yards and all this and that, they was like 'Well
maybe you can go; maybe you're going to college.' And then, by
the end of my eleventh-grade year, and when I started twelfth—
it's too late. I didn't have any advice—as a matter of fact, I had
more in my middle school at Cobb, right up here, to advise me,
you know, from those teachers, than at Leon, because they used
to come and see me and ask me how I'm doing—'Can we help
you in any way?' And when I was in high school, I used to think
about that—'How can these teachers from middle school still be
so interested in me?' In high school, it wasn't on account of my
citizenship, because my citizenship grades were good and I was
getting along well with all the teachers. I had teachers that loved
me to death, because I was sitting there listening to anything they
want they got to say; I wouldn't talk over them. More often, all
the teachers would rely on me—'Hey John, you sit there and you
were listening, even when I'm saying something wrong.' I was sitting there listening, because I want to learn. But they didn't have
that push, push.

"In twelfth grade, there wasn't much time for school, because
during that time I was only taking about four classes, because I

was pretty much close to having all my credits. I wasn't into school, that year. When I first started my twelfth-grade year, I knew I was going to get a scholarship; it started my twelfth-grade year, colleges writing me and sending me things. They first started calling me, writing me—I knew I would go then. If I'd have had someone to help me out, just a little bit of help, I'd have been in a little better shape.

"When I came to Florida State, I was just completely over my head. It was totally—it was total different English courses than in high school. In high school, it was—umm—pretty much your grammar. They pushed more to the grammar and stuff like that. Did I write much? See that's—that's what it was; we didn't—we went over different types of sentences and different things— verbs, adjectives—but as far as writing papers, I didn't write a paper in high school. When I went to Florida State, that was the first time of writing a paper. Five-hundred-word essay. What is that? In Leon—I didn't know what they mean. Book reports? Papers? No, nothing like that. I didn't never write, just straight out write, a book report—we would read, you know, books, and then go back and write down certain sentences that the teacher called out, and stuff—and that was it. But a thousand-word essay, a five-hundred-word essay—

"I think in high school, it was slow learning to me, 'cos things that we were going over, they would go over and over and over them again, just keep on over and over, and I guess that was for the people, some of the slower people in the class, but it was bor- ing; I don't know if it was maybe the teachers, or what their plan was, but it was difficult to go over the same thing. And I think what it is, they look at your grades, or look at the kind of work you do and then say 'Well, you need to be at this certain level; you don't need to try to a higher level'; it's like a mind game, you know—'That's high enough; you really don't need to go higher.' That's where I got caught, you know, they didn't try to push me *higher*; they just said, 'Well, you do this and make your grades and get your diploma.'

"I came straight out of high school and went straight to summer school at Florida State, and my English did bad, so my G.P.A. was down then before I even started ball; I took straight English right out of high school, right out as soon as I left Leon. Summer courses started and my dad paid for those out of his pocket, you know, that wasn't on scholarship. Really. That was just straight from him, you know, since I was pretty much wanting just to get into it then.

"You right. Not many parents would do that. Florida State didn't give me summer school. And I did want to go to summer school; I didn't want to stop school—I wanted to just stay fresh into it. I tried to get in early, to go ahead and take at least one English class, but I didn't have anyone to advise. And I didn't have any tutors, anybody to even *know* any college courses, so I was here writing papers myself, fresh out of high school, you know, I didn't know anything about writing papers for college. The best grade that I got in the summer was a C-plus; that was my best English, by myself—you know, I proofread it myself— that was the highest grade that I got, so that's where my G.P.A. dropped. Then when I started the regular semester, as far as English, it made me look like I was dumb as hell. If I hadn't have done that summer class, maybe I would have been at Florida State even longer than I was; maybe I wouldn't have been kicked out.

"The football office set my courses. I had a good history professor. See, that's why I did so good in history. My history was great. I enjoyed that. This professor, he would teach from an aspect of relating it to the future, or would relate it to today's time, and you could understand it, you know. I guess what goes around, comes around. He would have a parable, or have something to relate to what he was talking about. He would bring it around and maybe there would be a little sense of humor involved also, but he would make you understand and remember. So when you take the test, you can see it, clear, you know, it's just in your mind, you remember what he said, and you laughed, you know, story-wise. Yeah, it was like a class that I really enjoyed, so like I say, I aced that class and then math." He laughed. "That was a different story. English, you know, I finished English also. Pretty much history and math and English—people should take that more into consideration in high school, it would help more, I think I would be a whole lot better.

Wondering if he'd fared better at Leon than I had at my school, I asked him what kind of history he'd been taught in high school. The Civil War? African history? He shook his head.

"No, we didn't have that much of African history at all, at Leon. But then you go to the black teacher, she had a lot of African history. She would teach more African history than the white teachers, so that was her personal choice. But you know, I read a lot of black history and have a lot of black history books and stuff; a lot of students in high school didn't, but my parents, they would buy us—they would have black literature here, and history, that we could read coming up; it was exciting to look and see your own.

"After I left Florida State, I talked to different people and the dean of T.C.C. I was thinking to go to T.C.C., and get my A.A. and then go back to Florida State. T.C.C. isn't the same as Florida State, 'cos there is no one to help; I was here by myself. I got to get my own classes, my own place to stay—I moved back home, and that was it as far as Florida State. They didn't have anything else to do with me from the time that I went to T.C.C. My parents paid for T.C.C. Florida State didn't have anything—I asked them did they have anything they could give me, and they said no. So I paid for all that. They didn't offer even to try to help me, at any time. They said 'We can't pay for anything'; I'm all alone. It's pretty hard. But I tried. I tried, you know, to do good, but it's hard.

"I just go on, you know, push forward; but I need to and I am—like I say, I want to finish my A.A. I was trying to enroll for summer, but the summer is over now, of course; I think the nineteenth is the last date for T.C.C. enrollment. I can't keep putting it off and putting it off, because I know I can do it. I need about twelve or thirteen hours. I need humanities, science, and math. As a matter of fact, I *need* to go back to school; where I work with the county, they have an opening for an entomologist, and that's what I do. We have a program at the county that they will pay for that class. They pay one hundred percent for that.

"After F.S.U, everyone was like—'You not playing ball anymore? You sorry, or you this and that, or you dropped out,' or whatever. I think it was more my fault. I wasn't taught the system at all, but I think when my—when my self-esteem dropped, and my motivation dropped, that was it. I couldn't go on. I think—I don't fault anyone else, I fault myself. Because I had my goals, but I just let everything just . . . fall. I don't have any kids, I'm not married, so, you know, I'm not saying anything like relationships or anything stopped me. So I fault myself. I tried to go in and talk to Coach Bowden; he was busy, he would never come, he would never talk to me, you know, the only time he talked to me was at the end, when I was leaving. He would never—you could never talk to him. He would have his assistant say something to me.

"After I quit T.C.C., I didn't know what I wanted to do. I just—my mind was all cluttered up, 'cos I didn't know which way to go after then, you know, as far as going back and working with my father at the time, to try and make a little money. No one made me, pushed me, other than my parents. I worked different jobs, first with Lowe's hardware, then Coca-Cola; I did a little bit of restaurant work—I cooked and stuff like that, which was fine. I worked there at the Wedge and Wineglass—yeah, I worked there; just doing things, getting out in the world, finding out different things. I didn't want . . . I didn't want to—see, I didn't want to look at Florida State games.

"I'm more—not of a handyman, but I love doing things with my hands; I'm mechanically inclined, I guess that's what it's called. When I was coming up around here, people used to bring their engines and stuff over to my father and put them on the porch—'Reverend, if you get to it, do you figure you can fix this?'—and I would help him. After I left T.C.C., I did take a auto mechanics course. I didn't stay there but about two months, two or three months, then I decided I didn't want to make a career out of it, because the more I was starting to work on cars and be around them, I kinda was losing my hobby; and I just love to work on them. And then, I was off the deep, you know, hanging over a cliff, I didn't know which way to go. That's what I was trying to do—find a job that I enjoyed, that I liked.

"Now I enjoy my job with the county; I've been there about three years. I work with mosquito control. I go around, talk to different people. There's some people that *think* they know about mosquitoes, but they don't," said John, his eyes narrowing knowingly. "They're like, 'Well, it's just one mosquito in this area'; but it's *seventy-seven* different species—in Florida *alone*. Aaallll of different types, aaallll of different kinds," he said, stretching the words out lovingly. "They breed differently. I enjoy that. And I go to the courses in Gainesville and different places. I remember all—everything! You know, I just remember—we take a test, a hundred-question test, and I ace it. I get them all. I'm like, 'I'm not that smart, you know, but how could I do so well?' Because it's something I like to do. I think that probably if I *then* related to school like that, I would do a lot better, than letting my not playing football and the way they treated me break my ego down."

I realized as John spoke that I had never detected the full extent of the active curiosity behind his quiet, listening ways, and it occurred to me only now that of all the students in our group, he had probably been the one most interested in subjects for their own sake. His politeness had kept him from ever asking questions.

Down the corridor that connected the two houses, the sound of children playing could be heard coming from the kitchen. John's mother was an attractive woman, lean but strong looking, moving continually about the house, cleaning, fetching in laundry from outside, picking up children. In all the time I was with

John, she sat down only once, and then to cradle a toddler who had begun to cry. Her strong arms swooped children up easily, moved them from place to place—every motion she made was smooth, practiced, repeated many times over a lifetime. I imagined years of unruly life streaming through the house organized, tidied, instantly disciplined through Mrs. Feagin's maternal arts. I found it impossible to guess her age; her face was unlined if preoccupied, her hair covered with a floral kerchief. It struck me too that not only was she herself of indeterminate age, but she was *from* an indeterminate age—the age, perhaps, of the rural South twenty, forty years ago. From the vegetable garden outside, to the romping children within, everything in the Feagin home bespoke old-fashioned, homegrown values.

"My mother has always cared for children," said John proudly, "black, white—it don't matter.

"If I had kids, they'd go a different way than I did. I would pretty much push them more, as far as taking more college-level classes, as far as getting more prepared in ninth grade than I was. I think it makes a difference whether you *know* you're going to college. It does, it does. Because a lot of people that were in my class, for instance in Florida State, and they was asking 'Well, what's your major?' and they start 'undecided,' that kinda right there was showing me that they didn't really know which way they want to go. So my major was in communications. So I think more should be earlier, even earlier than ninth grade to say which way you want to go.

"Although lot of your young black guys that's coming up now, you can't tell them much. They think they're grown, they think they're grown. From being around a lot of my friends' young sons—seventeen, fourteen, fifteen, coming up—they think they're grown. Right then. You can't tell them much. I'm not saying that this hasn't been happening years and years back, but it used to be hey—you jump up and you talking back to your parents and something like that—you get your butt beat, right there. But now, it's guys talkin', talkin', you know. As far as my friends and stuff, they know that this kid here is really rude, or they know what's happening, but they let them just sit there talking—'Eff you' and 'I don't care about you'—little young kids! I think that's why I'm glad I don't have any kids, because I'd probably be in prison now for killing 'em." He laughed. "Or hanging 'em up in a tree. . . .

"I think that's what's happening with more of young blacks; a lot of them are like 'We can hang out, we can shoot, and we can fight, and we can even take. I'm a kid—they're not going to arrest me.' I've heard that from many young guys—'Hey, I do or I don't do what I want to. I steal a car, or do this and that—they're not going to arrest me. They can arrest me, but I'll be there for a day or two until my parents come'—and that's ridiculous. It's strange things happening.

"There's this club I used to go to—I don't go anymore. It used to be pretty nice, just laid back, you know, a nice club that you go in and have a few drinks and just have fun. But now young kids came up, and the owner he didn't call the police, or run them away. You got like sixteen-, seventeen-, eighteen-year-olds—anybody in there has a gun. I mean it's like, everybody—*everybody* has a gun. And there's no way I'm going near again. Really. He lets them come in—I fault the owner for that—he lets them come in and drink. I think the parents—some of the parents let 'em just do what they want to do; and then some work at night, you know, have different jobs. Just a lot of different things.

"I think the high schools could have more meetings, you know, as far as letting someone come and talk on their experience. That helped me when I was in high school. I wasn't the best kid—don't get me wrong, I didn't do bad things, but I was hanging out with different guys, and they're doing different things, and stuff like that. We had this guy come in, and he had been in prison, and he talked to us saying the things he been through and he would never want to go through them again. He was real strong-wise, mind-wise; it kind of made me think about it. That helped me a lot, a lot; I think the state system, or someone, should have—not prisoners, but ex-people that have experienced these things come in and talk to these kids in a serious way.

"When I first started driving, guys started taking things and picking up things that didn't belong to them, and putting them in my car, and I'm like—'Wait a minute. No! You're not going to do that'; that was the only fight—well I'll say it was the second fight—that I had in high school, when this guy brought a tape cassette that he stole out of a car and he was going to put it in my car. And the police came, saw him putting it in my car, and got my tag number and they called me down to the office and they read me my *rights*; they didn't arrest me, but they read me my *rights*. To make a long story short, the guy that put it in there, in my car, was my fast—one of my best friends, and he asked to use the keys to my car, because he said he had some clothes to put in; and he put in the cassette. From then on, I didn't have anyone riding with me. I used to leave for lunch; teachers knew, all the teachers up there knew; I was pretty much a pretty good kid, you know, I didn't have trouble.

"On TV, you know, it's all about guns—shooting and popping and zappin' things. All the music—everything they listen to is about shooting and poppin' someone, you know, with a gun or with a knife or something like that. I never thought of it; guns? Shooting and stuff? I never really—never really knew about that. But younger kids, too, now they're into games and different things around here a lot. I asked one of my friends' little boys—he's thirteen, he's about thirteen years old—I'm like 'How *could* you go around? You can't even go to the south side, or you can't even go to the north side or the west side of town—you can't just ride your bike.' Myself, I used to just ride my bike all over Tallahassee; I might go to Tom Brown Park, Easton Street—you know, these are two different sides. I just ride over. I might not know everybody from there, but I might know one or two people, a few other people—just meeting people, you know, just having fun riding my bike the whole day. Now kids can't do that, because they're frightened; they can't go on the south side—'I'm

on the north side of town, I can't go on the south side of town.'
And it's sad; it's sad, it's sad.

"I been in church all my life. I'm still in church. I'm on the
Usher Board—we do different things around church, you know,
taking up money; it makes me feel good. It's more young and
older women than young black men or older men; there are dea-
cons, and different older people that been in church a long time
and they're still going on, but there's very few guys in the church,
young guys. I tell a lot of the younger guys, 'The more you go to
church, the more you're gonna *want* to go to church; if you go
one Sunday and then the next three Sundays you don't go, and
the next four Sundays you go and the next Sunday—it's hard; it's
hard to stay into that pattern of going to church. I don't go to
church every Sunday, but I enjoy church. I like it; it's part of my
life. As a matter of fact, it's a big part of my life. And then round
my friends, they look up to that. You know, they say, 'Well, he's
going to church—John, how about me and you, you know, how
about us going to church with you one Sunday?' I say, 'It's fine,
no problem,' you know. So they enjoy it. They get into it, so it's
like a keeping-you-off-the-street thing, plus you're getting something out of it. You learn more, think more about different
things, different life, different parts of the community.

"I think it's not really just that a lot of your young guys, they
think they can't do better, or do anything else, I think it's more
they get the lazy laid back; they don't feel they have any obliga-
tion about anything. In your church, you gotta sit up and it's different. In our church, they have a mother—she's called a
mother—she comes around and if you're sitting laid back or
something she'll say, 'Hey, get up,' you know, 'Sit up straight,' or
'Don't chew gum,' or 'Don't talk'—they don't want the responsibility. They could be out on the street, standing out on the corner, and just hang out, you know, just be their own way—they
don't want someone telling them what to do, or they don't want
to live up to that.

"I thank the Lord I haven't been into any jails or anything like

that. Quent, Billy—at least I didn't go that way. I don't have anything—no worries in the world—but I love my freedom, and I
gotta have it. I must have it. And there's a lot of people locked in
jail—no way. I won't even go and visit with my friends; they say,
'Man, come with me.' No! I am not even coming to visit the jail.
It's easy to get into that system.

"Back to the time coming up here in Tallahassee—doors open
and just latching with a screen latch; all the windows up. You
can't do that now. It's hard. That's what made us get the burglar
bars," he said, waving an arm around the room. "A guy came in
here—he didn't know what he was looking for; he just took stupid stuff—lamps and chairs and Nintendo; little crazy stuff.
Grabbing! Just really stupid. So they got the burglar bars.

"This street is very quiet—they just started putting these
houses down there, on back; everything around us is owned by
the Hunters. That's why it's called Hunter Street. They gave
my dad that garden over here, and they gave him that spot. He
didn't know; they had that in the will, and he didn't know.
Everything around us is owned by the Hunters. They're a real
old, old family. I have my house over on the opposite side of
town; I just wanted you to come here so you could see where I
grew up and where my family lived."

It didn't take long, after leaving John, to make my way back
into the sweltering traffic and hard sights and sounds of Tallahassee. Passing Leon High, I remembered how it used to be the
last building of any note on Tennessee Street, which now extends
miles and miles beyond, where once there was only woodland, a
thruway off which weird, unknown satellite complexes have developed. I too could remember growing up in a quiet neighborhood, where windows and doors were kept open through the
summer nights. After leaving the house on Hunter Street, I better understood my old instinct that John had the air of a man
who came from another place; another place in time, I realized
now, not in space. In heart and spirit, he seemed more suited for
a quieter, gentler age.

DARRYL

When I first began to make inquiries about Darryl Gray, I was advised by the Football Office to get in contact with his "foster mother," Linda Jones, who lived in Tallahassee. This adoption program used to be run under the auspices of the Extra Point Club, an organization whose membership was drawn from the most devotedly loyal Seminole supporters. The club had recently lost its university-sanctioned status due to new N.C.A.A. legislation and exists now only on an unofficial basis. Players are no longer assigned to foster parents, as they used to be, although members can on an informal basis still invite individuals to their homes for "family" occasions.

I used to hear about this program when I was tutoring, usually when players were gearing up to spend an evening at their foster parents' home for dinner, occasions which some of my group used to find intimidating. I had never actually spoken to a "parent," however, and was momentarily as intrigued by the possibility of learning more about the arcane habits and customs of that curious entity, the hard-core football fan, as I was about finding Darryl Gray.

I was, then, almost disappointed to discover that apart from an excessive maternal instinct, Linda Jones appeared to be a perfectly normal woman. That she was genuinely fond of Darryl was apparent from the moment she opened her mouth. Proud of his accomplishments, she had followed his career closely since 1983, when she and her family had "adopted" him. Her family's continuing relationship with him was, by her own admission, a particularly happy one, and not at all typical.

"Foster parents had a place. It was not the one hundred moms of the Extra Point Club baking brownies before games that you had to worry about," she said ingenuously, "it was the people who came up after the game and pressed hundred-dollar bills into the players' hands. And that is always going to happen. A lot of the guys who come here are so bewildered and alone; many come from backgrounds that make it hard for them to adjust to apartment living. You cannot imagine the homes some of these guys have come from.

"Darryl was Greg Allen's roommate, and he had to have a lot of confidence to be so. Everyone was always calling on Greg—the press, women—there were always people calling. They were good friends; Darryl was best man at Greg's wedding, and I know they still stay in touch. Their apartment was as neat as a pin—it used to tickle me so. You wouldn't guess that they were football players. Their shoes were all lined up, they dusted, they had plants. . . .

"Darryl graduated and went straight to graduate school and got his master's degree. He has always worked, and he just keeps on striving and improving himself. He had good jobs after F.S.U. He was head officer in a correctional facility in Lewisburg, Pennsylvania, and then again in Memphis. Now he's an officer at a facility in Arlington, Texas, at the request of the warden. He's married and has a little girl; they lost the first baby, a little boy, at seven months. His wife almost died, and he grew up a lot in that short time.

"I still hold him as an example to my own children. I'm always telling them to look at what Darryl did."

* * *

In our brief conversation, Linda Jones had given me a more vivid portrait of Darryl than I myself had framed after working with him five evenings a week for just under a year. I remembered him as being large—bulky more than "cut," as the players would say of Greg or Billy Allen, for example—and having a round, smooth face and small, alert eyes. His manner had always been very businesslike, and he never wanted to play around or chitchat, and it was this matter-of-factness that had made it difficult to glean an impression of the individual behind the student. It was also the case that I worked with him for the most part on workbook grammar and not on reading or writing exercises, which would have entailed more discussion. Darryl used to sit hunched forward on the too-small chair by my table, his hands between his knees, intently but restlessly listening. Often, he would attempt to sum up or paraphrase what I had said: "OK, so what you're saying is . . ."

Because these summings up were not routinely one hundred percent accurate, I had at times thought that he was difficult to get through to; it was easy to forget that he was alone among the group in sticking his neck out, of risking public error, in the interest of getting it right. Darryl had not been one of the group's more colorful characters; but it now looked as if he might be one of the most successful.

"Yeah, I remember you—you had that . . . that accent. How're you doing?" said Darryl, when I called him in Texas. And then, "Me and my wife have just bought a home. You can stay with us when you come—no need to go to a hotel, Caroline."

Darryl met me at the airport with his little girl, Ebony. Apart from being darker from the Texas sun, he had changed very little since I had known him. His face was as smooth and unmarked as I had remembered it, his body as large and comfortably lumpy. By contrast, his legs and arms were slim and close to elegant, and the tapering, almost feminine beauty of his hands was particularly striking.

His little girl was a tall, handsome, scowling child of about five, with flashing eyes and a long imperious braid of hair, whose every willful feature indicated an implacable, headstrong nature. For all this, her scowl seemed to me artificial, part of a role she was playing, rather than an indication of real sullenness. She was both very indulged and very well disciplined, and I foresaw a long battle of wills ahead between her and her parents.

"Now Ebony," said Darryl, meeting her eyes in the rearview mirror as we drove to their home, to the accompaniment of her chatter. "You can see I'm talking. Don't think that just because we have company, you won't get a whupping."

Darryl's home was a spanking-new bungalow in a spanking-new housing estate. His house lay at the end of the estate road, and so had the temporary advantage of abutting as-yet-undeveloped land, an expanse of wild, high grass which in another place, on a more gently contoured surface and under a less harsh sky, one might have called a meadow. But this was Texas, a place for which gentle, idyllic words like "meadow" seem unsuited. This was merely raw, idle land, its marketable possibilities undetermined. In view of what I had begun to glean of Darryl, it struck me as significant that he alone of the group had been bold enough to launch himself far from his roots and family, out of Florida, out of the real South, out here, to make a new start. The garden plots that had been surgically sliced out of the flat wasteland, now to follow the coy curves of the estate road, were still not completely landscaped, and one could almost see the outlines of the squares of transplanted turf, the burlap sacking around the loosely rooted trees.

Inside, the house was perfect, as a frosted angel-food cake is perfect—fluffy, pink and white, immaculate. The white walls, the pale tan carpets, the pink-and-white curtains and chairs, the shining kitchenware—everything was new and inviolate. Later that night when I took a shower, I spent an age mopping up behind me, reluctant to sully with water spots the gleaming, seemingly never-before-used faucets and porcelain tub. Ebony's room was that of a young princess, with its tiny bunk bed, its child-size, bubble-gum-colored television set, its brand-new elaborate Fisher-Price miniature kitchen, complete with its tiny stove. There were also books, which Ebony brought in later to read— or rather to recite, as she had evidently learned them by heart.

While waiting for his wife, Lisa, to come home from work, Darryl settled himself in his new tan chair in the living room to talk; and while he did so, I found myself continually glancing around the room and the kitchen beyond, sensing in every detail the comfort and security and pride with which this brand-new whole had been assembled. Later, I would remember how Darryl described doing yard work for one of Florida State's more distinguished alumni as a weekend job, standing back in the garden, looking at the house and saying to himself, "One day. One day I'm going to have something like that."

"I didn't really have to try real hard in high school to pass. I mean, I guess I stayed away from the tougher classes. I would come home from school and my mother said, 'Go to your room and do your homework.' You couldn't tell her, 'I don't have no homework'—she wouldn't have believed that. I can't . . . I can't ever remember taking work home. Never. I can only remember, you know, studying for tests. So you went into your room anyway, stared at the wall, read a book—anything. My mother didn't finish high school, but she knew we had to get that education. I brought home a report card with bad grades and my mother said, 'No more basketball for you.' I cried for a whole day, I just cried. She said, 'If you bring your grades up, you can play.' I worked, I brought them up. I wanted to play that bad.

"It was the teachers who didn't care who you were, whether you were an athlete or not, you were going to do your work. Miss Smith, I'll never forget her. She was tough. For me, personally, it's a matter of being fearful of them, or knowing that if you did something wrong they're going to put you in deep trouble.

That's what it takes for somebody like me. Some kids, you don't have to, you know, make them—I say 'fear,' but I guess respect, and if you respect somebody I guess you do have a certain amount of fear, so to speak; but I think that's what it takes. Boys at the back of room, you know, we did nothing but laughing and giggling and going on, and she was one of the few black teachers that we had back then in something besides athletics—you know, a history teacher, who taught an important topic; as a matter of fact, maybe that's why I looked up to her; I seen, you know, a black teacher that I looked up to. She's the teacher that I remember. The English teacher, he was a white male, but he was another person that, you know, you in his class, he had a good class. It was one of those English classes where, I never forget, myself and another one of my friends we were—what were we reciting? Shakespeare! Shakespeare. 'Country—Roman; Romans and country . . . countrymen—Romans and countrymen, lend me your ear.' And we were doing that part, and everybody in the class was doing it, but me and the particular fellow that was working with me, Derrick Howe, he had a stuttering problem, but when we did that particular part, we did the best in the class; as a matter of fact, that teacher had—I think we went to the auditorium one day and he had everybody else sit down in the audience and listen to me and him do that part.

"Looking back, I definitely wish they had taught other subjects. A foreign language, you know, because I mean, all the other countries do it. I wish when I was coming up in high school there was—if there was, it wasn't required. It definitely wasn't required. If they didn't have it, I wished they would have offered it, made it mandatory.

"Also, I wished they would have taught—I won't say black history; I wished they would have taught more about history of all the different races, instead of the whole book being about, you know, just white America, or England—I won't say England, because in the history books, you know, the Europeans left England, and came here. More of a multiracial type deal, just teach history, you know, and not exclude one group or another group, just teach straight history. Now for me I had my mother, where she didn't talk about any black history, but she taught me pride. She, you know, gave me that self-esteem that you needed. My mother—we would see pictures, I mean every Saturday, Sunday morning, I'd get up and Tarzan—Johnny Weissmuller, I think his name—put Tarzan on, and see him over in Africa, man, and he would just—the Africans over there would just—he was king of everything. And my mother would always say 'Those are your relatives, your ancestors.' And I seen, you know, this white guy Weissmuller, and I'm like 'No they not!' You know, I want to be like Tarzan! 'No, they're not my ancestors. They ain't nothing but slaves'; that's exactly what I said. And she started laughing. She said, 'No, they're your ancestors.' You know, I was so mis-educated or whatever till I didn't want to have anything to do with them—that's all I thought black people did—run around in the jungle, no clothes, didn't do anything, you know, and then the white people came and taught them everything they knew, and pulled them up out of the jungle and all this and that—that's all I knew, and I guess it had some kind of effect on me 'cos I didn't want to be considered as being a part of African culture.

"Having the true history in the books about different things maybe would help some kids whose parents don't know about that. I hear a lot of people talking about it nowadays, about more African history or Hispanic history, and it's true that should be in there. But I also don't think it will work for kids by itself; what would help is, I guess, in the home, if somebody knew about being a parent. Now when my mother was coming along, I could say that maybe there was an excuse for her not knowing, but I think parents nowadays—*real* parents, not just teenagers, you know, real parents—if the school's not teaching it, they should be educated enough to teach it themselves. You know, at my job we have this every year, they be training us on cultural-diversity training. And I brought that up in the cultural-diversity class— try to get the books and teach your kids something. Go teach them yourself, don't wait for the school to do it, because if you wait for the school to do it, it may not happen, so go out and do it yourself.

"I never had any problem reading—I never had any problem with being able to read, but I guess because when I was coming up through elementary school, you had the teachers then, I guess, more so being teachers. I think a lot of kids, even before public school got integration, or whatever, you had to learn how to read and write, you know, because those teachers made them learn how to read, or worked with them, or took the time out; I think teachers loved doing their jobs then, you know. Kids weren't so bad, because the teachers knew if they told somebody's parent on them, the parent was going to take action. It was maybe as I got up to the high school level, I guess you could kinda see the change. As I got older, it seemed like kids were getting—not dumb, but just slower, and they say, 'Well the next teacher will get them' or something like that. But I was fortunate in elementary school to have teachers to work with me and help me. It's amazing how I look back on the teachers that I can remember, and I mean, I'm sitting here trying to remember a teacher, but every teacher that I've called out to you has been a black female: Miss Simmons first grade, Miss Carswell second grade, Miss Showers third grade—black females, and I had white teachers, but those are the teachers that stick out in my mind.

"We didn't do math past the ninth grade—I think we only did English through tenth grade—and when I got in high school, I *wanted* to continue to take math, you know, on up to precollege—I guess we took school more seriously, I think, when I was coming up; definitely now, if you give a kid an option of those tough courses—math, English, science—they're not going to take it. You know, if you can get a diploma, if you don't have to take it—hey! Shoot! Forget that. That's one thing I would change in today's schools.

"I guess by the time I got in high school I wasn't behind a lot as far as reading and writing. I know being an athlete, I got special privileges from some of the teachers, and a lot of other athletes, some of the big-name athletes on the team, I know they got special privileges from the teachers—because there was no other way they could have stayed. So it happened and it does happen, and you ought not to blame the cause on the teachers because the supervisors know about this, but they're concerned about winning games and have people coming to games, and making money for the school, and it's not like even if you had a teacher that probably wanted to say, 'Look, you know, this person just flunking,' I guarantee probably the time would come—'No, do what you gotta do to pass that person, or you not in this school, 'cos that person is making us win.' You know, we had some big names on our team—well, not my year, but the year before me, there were some big names. You know, I did the minimum just to go on to the next grade. Bottom of the problem is a system that's a shame—everything that you do is about the dollar. It seems like everything in this society, in sports, the bottom line is the dollar bill.

"When I got a scholarship to college, I was surprised, you know; when I was in high school, I was saying, 'Well, when I get out of high school, I'll go to the military.' That's what I was thinking. And when the college scouts started coming down watching me, I never realized I was good enough. Then I thought I'd do four years and get a trade and come out and start to work. That's what I had planned on doing. If not make a career out of football, go four years and come out. That's my plan, go to college, get a trade, and come out and work, or even make the military. Just as a way out, to have a job.

"There's no way of preparing. There is no way. Tell the truth, Caroline, when I got to F.S.U., I was scared, but then that first year, because, you know, the football team has academic advisers, that first year—hey! Did I even take—I took one core class, but shoot, I don't even remember. It was an easy schedule, you know, and I guess by doing that, maybe that eased my fears, or whatever, the next semester. I guess throughout the whole basic studies I wasn't afraid, but what I was afraid of was that other students in the class were so much at a higher level than I was at.

There was only one class I liked, that's the theater class I had, and in that I had a lot of people that I knew.

"I met Lisa at F.S.U. Matter of fact, when I met Lisa, that's when I—that helped my study habits, that helped me a lot, because when I used to meet her, she would always be in the library. If I wanted to spend time with her, I had to go to the library. Then since I had to go, I would start studying and picking up better study habits, and that really helped me out. Every time I would ask her out, she be, 'Well, I'll meet you over in the library.' Then when I started studying more, I started liking to go to the library, you know where it was quiet and you could sit down and and think—she changed my study habits a lot. Lisa got her degree in economics.

"In graduate school, that's what woke me up and made me realize—the classes were hard, but I wanted to go to those classes, for some reason. I . . . I got to where I wanted to study. It had to do with Professor Gertz, who stuck his neck out on the line and got me into graduate school. When I went to graduate school, I would write things and he would say, 'I want you to bring your paper over and make sure you write it properly' and this and that. I'll never forget, I took a paper to him and I had worked hard on the paper, and I took that paper to him and he got his little red marker, and he just went down that paper—'Nope, nope, good enough undergraduate, not graduate school, nope, nope, good enough undergraduate not graduate school, nope, nope, OK, nope'—and there were about three sentences left on the whole page that had no marks. And I'm like, 'What is going on?' He really opened my eyes up to what college was all about. Round when I was an undergraduate, I didn't know him, but I had enrolled in one of his classes, and on the first day he said, 'You will write two or three papers, you will read two or three books. If you do not want to do that, you need to leave this class.' And I bet you about half the students, including me, got up and walked out. Now, that was an undergraduate and he was a very demanding teacher. But I did finally take him. He used to let me go out to his house, if I wanted to get away, and go study there at his house. I didn't want to let him down, and I didn't. As a matter of fact, you never forget a teacher like that.

"When I was in graduate school, I would be in there with some of the teaching assistants going over the class work and taking notes, you know, going over class and the professor would walk by and see me in there studying. I was busting my butt, and I think I earned their respect; I think they realized I was not there for them to give me something, I wanted to earn it. And there were two classes I had to take those over; I made a C, and in graduate school you got to make an A or a B. I would talk to the professors after the class and say, 'OK, what do you mean here?' and so forth. I wasn't a smart student where I could just breeze it. I'm the type of person, I had to read it two, maybe three times to really get it down pat, and so you know, I just worked.

"Playing football, you get tired, and you don't want to study. It's hard. In graduate school, I didn't have to stay so late watching films some nights. I guess what a lot of athletes will tell you, if you are not prepared in high school, or on up, when you get to college, your time is short to study, you are not going—you are not going to make it. They can carry you through high school, but not, I guess, in college. You know, in high school we read *pages*; in college, suddenly the professor is saying 'Read chapter one through five.' I'd say, 'Gosh darn. One through five? There's only twelve chapters in the book. Why we reading the first five in two weeks?' In high school, we never read more than a few pages, and then you knew the teacher would go over them in class. In college, the professor would be saying you got to read this book, but we won't be covering it in class—you know, read this book and we're not even going to talk about it? They'd tell you, write a research paper. Research paper? In high school, we never wrote anything like that. And it's not just because the work is harder in college, it's because you're on your own. It was up to you. That's where the discipline you got at home helped. You know, you never had classes back to back; there was time in between. And you had to be disciplined to use it.

"When I first got there, after I seen all the work of football—time I got this, and the time I go here, and time I go to practice—I didn't want to practice, I was tired, I just wanted the whole thing to be over with. Tired of football and tired of school. I was never hoping to go to graduate school. But a friend of mine, he said, 'What? This professor gonna help you get to graduate school and you're not going to go? Man, I wish someone would give me that kind of opportunity.' And, you know, it was that little talk, and I said, 'Well shoot, maybe you got a point.' Beside being scared that I couldn't do the work, I had planned on going trying out for U.S.F.L. when they were allowing, but that was only to maybe one or two years, to get money to buy me a house, just outright, down payment on a house, and that was it.

"That's one of the reasons why, before I knew I was going to Florida State, I said when I get out of high school, I was thinking I would go to the military, 'cos guys—I would see guys stand on the street corner, or just go to the gym and play basketball. A lot of them would have jobs, but it would be jobs—you know, guys down in Florida, a lot of the orange juice and stuff, they supply for. In my hometown, that's what you did in the summertime a lot, and it was something I didn't want to do. You know, there was no way I was going to be working in a citrus field—we call them groves—there was no way I was going to be doing that the rest of my life. A person that's a drug abuser or an alcoholic looks a lot older than what they are, and to me that's what picking fruit does. I'm glad I did it during the summer, because it made me realize—that was the number-one thing; and the second thing was seeing older men in my community, men get old and not have anything to show for it—it's not one of those things, any type of worthwhile occupation.

"The town I came from is called Lake Wales, but my family lived out in a little—I guess, suburb—called Babson. It was three streets—it was a black community—and it was just three streets out in the middle of a grove, you know. But we went to school in

Lake Wales and everything, it was just one of those communities
I guess they build about maybe four or five miles from the town.
I picked fruit to have some money coming in, and I'd be able to
help my mother. I did it up until, I guess, I got in high school,
and then I started working at a grocery store, as a bag boy.

"It was my uncle, my grandmother's brother—I can't say
enough about him. He was the one besides my mother that always instilled in me put something back for a rainy day, no matter, a dollar or whatever it is, because you never know, he always
say you never know. When I used to go to the grove, he would
go out there—he had retired, and he was an older gentleman, but
he would go out in the grove with me, and we would pick, and I
mean he would give me a hundred percent or ninety-nine percent of whatever he picked. I was younger, I could pick faster
than him, but still by him being out there, that was a big help.
He, I guess, took the place of my father, when my father and
mother broke up, because he taught me a lot, he really did. Even
though, you know, the same principles that he taught me, these
were the same principles of my grandmother, naturally; she was
also, she was always there. I think she probably saw him spend-
ing a lot of time with me, so she was more into my sisters, more
of a mother figure to them. Maybe a couple of summers, my
mother would go up North and pick apples, and we would stay
down there with him, I used to go and work in the grove with
him. Before he retired, he had an occupation where he would
drive the tractor down the aisles of the grove and they would
spray pesticide on the trees to keep bugs away—that's another
thing I didn't want to do. You come home every day smelling like
pesticide—that's something I didn't want to do, but I used to go
there with him.

"The neighbors in the community—the Bronsons, the Chad-
wicks, the Thompsons—everybody was just there to tell on you,
or whup you, or whatever, discipline, whatever needs to be done,
to make sure you stay in line. Everybody in that community that
came up with me, and definitely before me, at least finished high
school. The people who went to school with me, in my commu-

nity, it was almost as though finishing high school was like finishing college. Seemed like it was that important; it was like you did whatever you had to do to finish high school.

"Even back then, I think teachers may have been scared of the students—but then you had those teachers who were not afraid of the students, and if you had more teachers like that, and that would tell the students, constantly keep pounding their heads, beat it in their heads, plan for a career before they finish high school and go down a one-way street. Now I had that coming to me at home, so I guess I didn't need it in the school, but a lot of kids don't, they don't have that coming from home. Their counselors maybe should ask, 'What is it that you want to be? What do you want to do when you get out of school?' Try to have some type of structure that lets them start preparing for that goal; have people—not professional athletes, but everyday working people—come into the school, because that's the careers that people are going to eventually take; everyday working people would be the people that would help you find the job that you'll have when you finish high school or finish college, or whatever. My church has a group of us, members of the community, who get up and talk. The pastor said, 'These men here probably earn between them a quarter of a million dollars a year.' He wanted the kids to know that it wasn't just the athletes, but the businessmen, the middle class. Students see other people dressed nice, or whatever, come into the school, instead of just athletes on TV; find just everyday working people; let people from law enforcement come in and let them know—'Look, this is what's going to happen to you if you don't get a job.' I would even—naturally, it would have to be monitored—have an inmate come in: 'Look, I chose this path, and look where I am. You're not going to make it without an education.' They'll talk to you about how most of the inmates are criminal black males, but the majority of them have no education either. The majority of them have, I mean definitely not college, but I'm saying not even high school. Education—I mean, it's . . . it's education and crime or whatever, I think they go hand in hand. There's some kind of relationship.

"For blacks, the starting line where they start out is behind where the white students are at, so to speak. But I don't agree with lowering the test standards, or whatever, because all other countries are raising their test standards. In graduate school, I was behind, starting out, I was not a 3.0 student. I was behind, but I caught up by working my butt off, and I mean I had to work. Japan and the other countries are raising their standards, and what you're going to have is a third-world country here, and that's a sad situation. That just doesn't hurt blacks, whites, that hurts America. Now, if you got a problem with the test, what you need to do, lobby to have blacks in the room to help make the tests, you know, lobby for their participation, but don't lower the standards. Because, see, what's going to happen, when I get ready to retire, you're going to have a generation of people that's not going to know what to do.

"You know, I learned nothing at all that I remember at the undergraduate level. That's it—you get your degree, and your employer is going to train you for your job anyway. It's not going to matter what you did to get your degree. And yet, you know, we throw people away because they do not have college degrees. I know that in Germany, they have a system where they train you for a trade; they still do things with their hands, over there—plumbing, electricity, that kind of thing. They invest in their people, they train them right and make them competitive. It doesn't matter that they don't have that degree. The system here has become so money hungry that they don't want to invest in the people, you know, companies don't want to retrain, spend the money to retrain people where you need to retrain them, because that takes money out their pockets. They don't want to reeducate their workers to stay competitive in the workplace. We are a service nation—you know, like how a third-world country's only industry is tourism? We are only a service nation, we do not produce anything. In terms of education, everyone is ahead of us. They are educating more and more, and we are just going downhill. The entertainment industry is the only thing we can compete in. And that's because other countries don't choose to excel in that. Fine, Japan has a baseball team and so forth, but that's not what they choose to be a world leader in.

"It's got to the point now where parents and schools have got to work together. Like with Ebony now, as a matter of fact, in day care, where she starts to school, that's one thing—every meeting they have, I'm going to be there. As a matter of fact, I'm going to be going up generally to school and every class she has. I want to know what kind of book she's reading or what kind of textbooks they use; I want to be a part of it, I want to be a part of her educational experience. That's one thing that my mother as a parent—she didn't go to P.T.A. meetings, she didn't do a lot of that. I will go out there and voice my opinion, just to let them know I am a conscientious parent, and a concerned parent. I don't want my child just to come to school and just go over a test—you know, I want her to be taught. That's what people are paying tax dollars for. So I find myself thinking a lot of times that it helps them to maybe spend more time getting books, start looking at words and stuff, right now. Lisa has worked with her a lot on her writing. Right now, she kind of writes her name backwards. What do they call it? Dyslexia? She'll write letters backwards. She will know a lot about African history, 'cos she'll be reading some books. Me and Lisa would love to go to Africa; we plan to go in maybe the next five years."

Darryl's wife, Lisa, had come in while we were talking and after greeting us had quietly gone about preparing dinner. She was a handsome, powerful-looking woman, who had run track at Florida State. Here in her new home, her every action betrayed a kind of daunting adult competence, as if she had all her life known exactly what was required to be a wife, a mother, to run a household and hold a full-time job—already a woman who would be approached for advice in her community. She harbored, one sensed, strong, stern opinions, based on hard realities already confronted. Lisa worked with the local social services, handling child-support cases, and I felt a certain vicarious satisfaction in picturing to myself a delinquent father's attempt to explain himself out of her corner.

Darryl worked as a safety officer within the federal penitentiary in Arlington, his job being to monitor all aspects of the facility for potential safety hazards. I accompanied him to work the
next day, and it was while walking beside him as he strode into
the premises that I fully realized what a role model he could be,
or had become—a strikingly tall, good-looking man, in an immaculate official uniform, respectfully greeted by everyone he
met as "Mr. Gray." The "facility" itself contrasted dramatically
with the others I would visit in the course of this project, pos-
sessing, with its neat lawns and flower beds and cheerful brick
buildings, something of the air of a country club. Inmates were
engaged in furniture construction, tailoring, and maintaining the
gardens. The bright, airy dormitories were how I imagined (without ever having seen one) a junior tennis camp would look. Returning from the dorms, we passed a man who was pretending to
clean a large window while watching an exercise class conducted
by a bouncing model on the monster television screen. With the
kind of material backgrounds the inmates typically come from, I
could not help thinking, induction into the federal penitentiary
system must, in terms of lifestyle, represent a kind of upward mo-
bility.

"I had a shock when I first got into the prison system," Darryl
had told me while we sat talking in his home that first night. "I
had not realized the situation, how bad it was, of the black male.
I guess a lot of athletes, they come up through high school being
sheltered from really knowing how things are in the black community. Blacks are only eighteen percent I think it is of the population, but we are fifty, sixty percent of the prison population.
Because I'm black, you know, I get people, inmates, come up,
'Bro, help me.' But I always ask, 'What are you in here for?' 'Oh,
I was in the wrong place at the wrong time'; 'Oh, it wasn't much.'
I say, 'Was it drugs? And who did you sell to? And where did you
sell? In your community? You are killing your own, selling to
kids—don't "bro" me.' I'm hard on them. They tell me, 'I got
tired of seeing my mother work. I wanted to help my family.' I
say, 'Oh—and how are you supporting your family here? How

are they living while you're in here? You know, if you're in on a drug charge, the government can take *everything* away. So how are you supporting them now?' They try to lay this down on me—'You got a job because of us.' I say, 'We need you on the outside. And if there were no prisons, I'd be doing something else. I'd flip hamburgers at McDonald's to support my family.' They say, you know, that they see other people driving these cars, having these things, and they want them, quick and easy. They tell me, 'I'd have to work my whole life to buy that.' I say, 'And what's *wrong* with working day after day? What's wrong with that? Everybody in the world is not going to be rich—any religion tells you, you got the widow, the orphan, and the poor. Everyone in society is not going to be rich.'

"The people in prison I meet, they didn't have—I think a majority of them didn't have a real father, not a real man. Therefore, when they have kids, they can't teach their kids how to be responsible, how to be a man, how to be serious about their education, 'cos *they* don't have education. As a matter of fact, the majority of the guys, all they want to do is have kids from maybe two or three different females—they think that's being a man. And it's not. Having a lot of kids is not being a man, raising them is.

"In today's society, especially within the black community, kids are parents—they're raising themselves while they try to raise their kids. You know, being a parent is not being a friend to your kid, it's not, like, doing the same things together. You are there to teach them right and wrong, so that they will know. It's hard to discipline them at times, but you are not doing them any favors if you don't. In my church, I work with young kids, take them on camping trips, you know, programs which give them a male figure in their lives. I got up in church and said, 'If you want to come and play around and just have fun, go somewhere else. I will not be here to be your friend. I am here to be an adult to you.'

"Now it's my—I believe before, when we didn't have any-

thing, you know, in the period before integration—when we became integrated, we worked so hard to become integrated, we
became integrated, we thought that what we were doing is wrong
and we're integrated now, so we need to change and do what
white society is doing. And I think that really hurt. I think that is
why now today in the educational system a lot of blacks fail. Before we were integrated, our kids, they had their school. And
they were being taught. And when we became integrated, we
took our kids out of the classrooms where they were being taught
and shipped them somewhere else, to another environment
where maybe they didn't feel comfortable, felt alienated and
were not the same type of students that they were at their own
school. And I really think what we was doing before integration,
when we became integrated, we thought it was wrong. You
know, the extended family—in my community, if you was out
after dark, people, your neighbors, would say, 'Get home. You
know what your mother is going to do if she finds you out here.'
When the sun set, we were inside. In my community, my folks
would come with a switch to switch you down the road, embarrassing you in front of your friends. But when we were integrated, as far as discipline, we wanted to discipline like how
white Americans discipline, whatever way that was, and it may
work for them, but for our kids, it didn't work.

"I do believe—and integration by no way is bad, but I think
that's what happened. I think that when you hear a lot of blacks
talking about economic empowerment. Before integration, we
had our stores, our own cleaners and everything, but when we
became integrated, everybody left that, moved in other neighborhoods, and those stores went out of business and we started
taking our business elsewhere—because when we say 'integration,' we're the only one that integrated, you know, we don't
have the white kids coming to our schools, our businesses, inte-
grating two ways.

"Today employment in the black community is worse than it
was before integration. It has to do with, you know, we were hir-

ing our own, we had our own businesses, and we were hiring our own then. When we became integrated we left that and tried to get jobs in the white community. They weren't ready for integration, and maybe a lot of people still aren't ready for integration, but if you have your own economic base, you can support yourself, like a lot of the Jewish communities, Chinese communities do—you can support yourself. Whereas we went to the white American community, and you know welfare, that came on—it destroyed, I think, our family values that we had. In the black community, if you have somebody—I've always had a problem with this and this is what I mean by low self-esteem, you know, not feeling good about yourself—the community is still, I believe, miseducated so that if they have a child and the child's hair is not long and stringy, they're still like—'Your child got nappy hair, ooh, look at the child's hair.' It's nothing against white America, or anything, because they didn't tell us to change—but once we became integrated, we thought we had to change, we thought we had to look like them, dress like them, raise our kids up the way they did. And you can't. If that's the way white America raises their kids, it works for them, but you can't stop raising your kids the way you raising them; coming from Africa, you going to hand stuff down till it come to your parents, and all of a sudden, what was working, you just stop doing it.

"You know, I watched the Tony Brown Journal, talking about how people are like—'There's no money in the black community.' The black community, if it was a country, would be the ninth-richest country—yeah! or something like that; I know in the top ten. We make money, but then we spend ninety-five percent of it in the white community; and when we spend the money in the white communities, we leave our communities, and then we wonder why our community is poor. See, it's not all about— I'm not just saying this because you're white and you're here. It's not all about white people keeping us down; a lot of it has to do with blacks putting money back into their own community. And every time me and my wife go out, I know she probably get tired of me always bringing it up, but to restaurants and stuff, you know, if I know of a black restaurant that sell the same—'Look, let's go over here and eat at this black restaurant,' not that I'm trying to be prejudiced, or anything, but I guarantee you, you not going to have a lot of white people go into the hood, you know, they're not going to take a chance of going over there and getting robbed, or jumped on, or whatever, so it's up to us to give them business. The churches—that's the only institution the blacks have is the church, and, you know, the churches collect a lot of money on Sunday from the black people—but they'll take their money and go to a white bank. Now if you—if all of these blacks, and if black I guarantee you going to have churches, all these black churches have these preachers, why can't they take their money, pool their money together, and start a black bank? For some reason, we don't want to work with each other. I think that's what the Black Panthers and the Muslims were trying to get a lot of black people to see, you know, be proud of who you are; and I think because they were doing that they got a bad rap of being violent, and so forth. Muhammad Ali, he was the great one. He may not know to this day how important he was—and everybody loves him still; no matter what race you were, everybody still loves Muhammad Ali. He just had, I mean, he could say things that an ordinary person couldn't say, and he got in a position to do that—and he did."

It was past midnight when Darryl and I stopped talking—how was it I had never detected this intellectual fervor in the eighteen-year-old I had tutored more than a decade ago? Having said good-night to him and Lisa, I turned into my room, then some moments later came out again to get a glass of water.

"Oh, I'm sorry," I whispered, and turned back, glad he hadn't heard me. For Darryl was on his knees before the sofa in the living room, his big round back hunched away from me, saying his prayers before going to bed.

BILLY

Billy was not, properly speaking, one of our group. He came to study hall at the same time we met, however, and as the weeks passed, he slowly drifted over to our circle, where he would usually sit and observe what was going on, while doing his own work. Billy was older than all the other players, and alone of the group was not from the South. His age was an obvious butt of many jokes: "Now you just take your twenty-six-year-old self away from here. . . ."

He had joined the air force straight out of his high school in Cleveland, and he told me once that this had been his salvation, that most of his high school friends were dead, from drugs or killed on the streets by each other.

Because he was older, because he had seen the world, and because he was good-looking and charismatic, Billy was a leader, and a conspicuous member of the team as a whole. In study hall, one could watch him make his way slowly across the room, stopping to chat or joke with everyone on the way, squeezing the flesh and working the room like a politician. If the Tallahassee *Democrat* ran a large, colorful, and touching photograph of one of the F.S.U. players signing a little boy's jersey, as likely as not the player would be Billy Allen.

In many ways, Billy did not, in fact, really strike one as being a student. He exuded worldliness, and one sensed a whole big life out there beyond his study hall and classroom appearances. Billy had come to F.S.U. in an unorthodox manner. In 1978, Coach Bowden had been in Europe, touring various U.S. service bases on the lookout for hidden talent, and in England he heard about a sensational player who was breaking all service records. Bowden never saw Billy play, but bumped into him one day as Billy was returning from a jog and told him to look him up at Florida State when he got out of the service. Billy took Coach Bowden at his word and turned up in Tallahassee two years later, initially as a walk-on, but by his second year on scholarship. He also ran track and eventually went to the National Championship as the second man on the school's 4 x 100 meter team. Recruited as a running back, Billy was overshadowed by Greg Allen, and he was often frustrated by what he perceived as the scant time he saw in action. Still, it was Billy who, in 1982, set the Gator Bowl record for a touchdown run—ninety-five unmolested yards down the length of the field.

It was clear that Billy had gravitated to our circle in part because of a kind of curiosity about me. Since he could not intrude on the time allocated for study hall, he arranged matters with the authorities so that I met with him for regular tutoring sessions, one-on-one. Usually we met at one of the tables under the big live oak tree outside the library. Sometimes, he would pay a visit to the swimming pool, where he knew I worked out with an informal "team" at noon. Wearing nothing but very short canary-yellow satin running shorts, mirrored glasses, and his Walkman, he would call out and beckon over the chain-link fence until I came, self-consciously, across the strip of intervening grass, over to him.

"Everybody's looking at you," he would say, flashing his million-dollar smile. "Everybody's wondering what's going on."

Billy liked to discuss, and he liked the give-and-take of a real argument, of breaking down his opponent's logic. His dress, his flamboyance, the fact that he moved within a shoal of women—

all of these characteristics could lead one to take him as a light-
weight, which in some ways he could be, and in his slickest
modes his speech was painfully glib; but usually in our discussions I would eventually stub my toe on the bedrock of his highly
astute intelligence. Billy could win arguments because his point
of view was unexpected and one had not previously prepared
counters for it, as one does with conventional presentations, and
because he had an air of confidence, even authority, that could
seduce one into believing he must be speaking the Truth. His instinct for other people's psychological makeup was real, however—an additional advantage—and in his matter-of-fact
exposure of this knowledge he could be ruthless.

"You are a very strong, very intelligent woman," he told me,
on the day after I had dropped off a book that he had asked for
at his apartment, on my way to campus. "But there is something—something *weak* about you. I knew, yesterday, that I
could have taken physical advantage of you in my apartment," he
said looking me dead in the eyes. "I knew that you would have
been too—*embarrassed*—to say no; it wouldn't be *polite*. I'm
going to tell you something; you've got to learn to say 'I do not
want a sexual relationship.' Say the words—'sexual relationship.'
Otherwise some nigger's going to be pretending that he don't
understand what you mean."

We briefly corresponded while I was in Africa: "Now, as for
school," he wrote in the same matter-of-fact tone with which
he exposed others, "my books are kicking my behind." My memory was that Billy was majoring in communications. I had no
idea, for all our talks, what he really intended doing: I could both
picture him doing everything he talked about, and nothing. For
his part, however, whatever it might be, he knew his future
would be dazzling.

Skidding one hand off against the other, so that it pointed into
the air, he would tell me, "I'm shootin' for the stars."

*   *   *

The Frank Scott Correctional Institute lies outside Milledgeville, Georgia, some four hours south of Atlanta by road. Milledgeville is a small, genteel southern town, with a redbrick women's college and old white wooden houses lying off its side streets. The town has two claims to distinction: it was the longtime residence of Flannery O'Connor and was briefly, at the outset of the Civil War, the capital of Georgia; it was Billy who told me this latter fact, adding that "the Civil War almost destroyed this little town."

The prison—or "facility," as I learned to refer to it—lay some miles from Milledgeville, beyond a manicured no-man's-land that formed a buffer zone between it and the town. An expanse of rural land such as this, particularly in a steamy summer in southern Georgia, should have been a mass of tangled overgrowth, and the fact that the road rolled tidily over dipping, apparently groomed hills betrayed, even on the outskirts, the unmistakable imprint of a controlling Authority. Appearing at the end of this protracted driveway was a large complex of old brick buildings with tiny windows, ponderous and Victorian in character and set back some distance behind surrounding high fences surmounted with rolled barbed wire.

The reports I had at first obtained, when I began to make inquiries as to Billy's whereabouts, were various. I knew that he had been drafted to the New Orleans Saints—and that his stay with them had been inexplicably brief. I knew he had come back sometime afterward to Tallahassee. Some people told me he was modeling in Miami; some that he had been seen selling drugs in Frenchtown, an economically poor and predominantly black quarter in Tallahassee. Others said that he had gone to Atlanta, where he had started a cleaning business with a friend. It was entirely characteristic of Billy that all of these reports seemed plausible.

Eventually, I was told to contact Curtis Thomas, also a former F.S.U. player who had gone on to the pros, and a friend of Billy who had known him in Atlanta. I called him one evening, introduced myself, and told him I was trying to get hold of Billy.

"Oh, you can get hold of him all right," said Curtis. "Billy had some problems with drugs. He's . . . ah . . . in prison."

Curtis had, like Billy, been a walk-on at F.S.U. "They call us walk-on, peon, piss-on," said Curtis, "so we had a lot in common. Getting a scholarship, to me, was like winning an Oscar."

Curtis had his own views of what had gone wrong: "Limelight was the major thing that excited Billy. The excitement of sports—it carried over into life. And when the sports were gone, he found that excitement dealing drugs—I'm not saying I would do that, but I can understand something of why he did it.

"Billy had been a defensive back in New Orleans. He was a running back at F.S.U. That shows you how much talent he had, to convert from offense to defense. What happened? You have to ask. I talked to him about it, but he didn't tell me everything. But you don't go from third-, fourth-round draft, and then no one takes you. Only five percent of college players make it in the pros. Something went wrong.

"He gave power of attorney to some agent, and he got fleeced by some agent or lawyer. There's all that legal jargon in the contract, and you have never negotiated anything. You trust the agents; he's telling you he's represented this guy and that guy, who did this and that—you have to trust them. All his money is gone. There was the agent that took advantage of him, legal fees . . . he's in until December of 1994, so he's still got some time.

"I have friends who joined the marines. They were in Singapore, Germany—when you play ball, you think you're on national TV. Uh-uh. You're across the world. Friends of mine in Japan and Germany saw me in a bowl game. Playing in the pros was one of my greatest fulfillments.

"Perhaps when you've talked to Billy, you'll want to do my story. Just kidding."

I had spoken to Billy several times at length on the telephone before I made this visit. As inmates are not allowed to receive telephone calls but can only place them (collect), I had left my number with his counselor, expecting to hear from him in a few days' time, if I was lucky. Instead, within five minutes of my hanging up the receiver he called.

"So, look where you find me," he said, but with all the old energy and optimism in his voice. It took little encouragement for him to plunge into his story.

"After college, after, you know, the pros didn't work out, I got into some trouble with drugs. I'm in here for trafficking. November twenty-fifth, 1991, I came here. August, I was in a holding center in Jacksonville, a processing center where they figure out what they want to do with you.

"I had a number of jobs and everything I did, I did *well*; but I just wasn't . . . I kept looking for more. Dealing drugs, I could make five thousand dollars in five minutes."

He had been, as he said, "into material things" and twenty-four-hour partying, as Curtis had told me. Breaking a cardinal rule of the drug trade, he became an addict. During this time he was also "seriously" involved with two women, each of whom bore him a son. One woman was roughly his age and lived in Atlanta with her mother, who was, as Billy said, "good people." The other was a teenaged girl he met at a club.

"She was supposed to be at least twenty-three. I moved her in, moved the furniture in, and basically told her to sit. After she got pregnant, I talked to her mother, who was going to fly down to meet the man her daughter was living with. Her mother said, 'My daughter's very young,' and that's when I found out. Before, I had just noticed that she didn't handle problems well—she'd just withdrew. I never took the time to speak to her, so I never knew her well. I had about four ladies I was taking care of at the time."

This much came from the Billy Allen I had known. When he talked about his past, he spoke in the language I recognized. By contrast, when he talked about what he was doing now, in prison, he had a whole new vocabulary of phrases: "positive attitude," "negative attitude," "definite major purpose," "master-mind alliance," "constructive use of leisure time for self-enhancement." At certain points, usually when talking most passionately, his newly acquired vocabulary literally broke down, and he fumbled for words before resorting to his old voice. On more than one occasion, he referred to a book called *The Science of Success*, by Napoleon Hill, which was clearly a guiding light in his new life. He was also "born again." He was an instructor in a recently developed prison program, Prisoners Helping Prisoners, which, as I gathered, was aimed at transforming negative mental attitudes to positive.

"Girl," said Billy, toward the end of our second conversation, "when you coming to visit me?"

"What's your schedule? How do you do it?" I asked.

"You have to come anytime on the weekend. But see, where I'm at—I'm . . ."

I anticipated. "Let me guess. You're booked up."

"Naw. I ain't booked up. What you mean booked up? Girl, what you mean booked up? I got a lot of people coming to visit me? No. No, this has been—I got a lot, Car—I—it has been— I'm gonna tell you, this has a been very . . . very"—he laughed— "interesting point. I mean I haven't had, I have had, since I've been locked down, two visitors. And both times they have been my son, and his mother and her mom.

Before signing off on our last conversation he said something that took me by surprise.

"The only thing I dreamt of was the pros." It now seemed so obvious, but I had never known it was of this he had been dreaming: I suppose I had thought it was of being a sports announcer, an advertising executive—something. I had never known that this was what he meant by "shootin' for the stars."

At the visitors' entrance, I stood behind a young woman who had already been turned away twice that morning for infringement of the dress code. She had traveled far to see her boyfriend and was wearing an attractive and obviously new red halter dress.

"Don't you have *anything* with you to cover up?" asked the guard, brotherly but exasperated. I was screened and let in, and when I next saw her, she had a towel draped across her shoulders.

The visiting area was an anonymous room with shiny linoleum tiles, one or two folding tables, and the kind of auditorium-style metal chairs that are expressly designed to preclude comfort. The only other features of any note were soft-drink and candy-bar machines—Billy had specifically instructed me to bring change. Disconsolate couples and one family were scattered around the room, sitting for the most part, strikingly, in silence; in my rapid survey, I discerned only one conversation. The inmates were dressed in white shirts and trousers, with blue stripes down the leg, and if hadn't known better, I would have assumed I had walked in on the lunch hour of a company of off-duty janitors.

A door at the back of the room opened and in walked Billy, ahead of a guard, the picture of vibrant, uncontainable health. His hair was clipped short, which suited him, and he was wearing trendy-looking shaded glasses. He wore the requisite white uniform like a tracksuit, bulging out of it at every seam: as he would tell me later, one of the ways in which he utilized his leisure time for self-enhancement was by long sessions in the weight room. He stooped to say a few words to the guard in a manner that suggested paternal benevolence. It struck me as almost ludicrous—particularly when contrasted with the other dispirited inmates—that the kind of food I knew he must be eating and the kind of air I knew he must be breathing could produce such preposterously healthy results.

Billy smiled happily when he caught sight of me, showing no discomfort at being encountered in these surroundings. Ostentatiously, he began asking the guard for directives.

"Can we sit at this table? Can we take these chairs over here? OK over here? She needs something to write on." I remembered Curtis's comment that Billy loved the limelight.

"It's been a long time, hasn't it? It's been a long time. It's been a *long* time. Well—let's see. You've held up pretty well. Your hair is different—it's darker and not all *sticking* out like it used to. You always had all that chlorine in it. Your weight looks about the same. You still swim? You still keep in shape?"

He next asked me to join in prayer with him, to give thanks for this occasion. "I should have done it before, but I forgot." Then he turned his attention to business. "Now, you've come here to do a job, so don't get carried away and forget your purpose."

Like several of the other players, Billy looked back on a particular event or period at F.S.U. as a negative turning point in his life. In this case, he felt the fact that Coach Bowden had not let him play defense, which is what he had been practicing, had deprived him of a good junior year, thus hurting his chances when it came to the draft.

"I thought of quitting, but I hung tough." Nonetheless, in 1985 he was drafted to the Saints, in the fourth round. He played until the next-to-last exhibition game, at which point he was cut.

"I was playing and training for many positions. I played strong safety, nickleback/defense, kickoff unit—block or punt return—kickoff return unit—so I know it wasn't because of performance. I think my agent was pushing too hard for too much quick money, instead of nurturing my career and looking after my long-term interests, and they got tired of it and just cut me off." But he also said of this time, "I was into everything, except my primary purpose. Except playing football. A year later, I ran into Alphonso Carreker—you remember him? He's with Green Bay. He told me that Coach Phillips in New Orleans had been trying to reach me, but I never knew.

"I can look back now, Caroline, and know exactly when I went wrong. Right after I got drafted, I dropped my guard. I allowed others to do for me. I allowed others to do my thinking for me. My agent did all the negotiations."

Billy had been fairly close to graduation when he left F.S.U. for New Orleans, needing only twelve credit hours and an internship to get a B.A. in advertising—apparently, communications had fallen by the wayside. Then, after his failure in the pros, he returned to F.S.U., in December of 1985—still on a football scholarship.

"Is that what you ended up getting your degree in?" I asked. "Advertising?"

He leaned back in his chair and grinned. "Criminology."

After graduation, he had a series of good jobs: as a correctional officer in Tallahassee; as an investigator of misdemeanors in the State Attorney's Office.

"That was fun," he said, "that was figuring people out." He had started drinking on his return to F.S.U., as well as making his drug connections.

"I moved in two worlds. Through my contacts at work, I met senators, the governor, professors from school. Then I had my life in the streets. I did it for the thrill of it. I liked the power, you understand. I liked seeing what I could get away with."

This job lasted for only three to four months, and in July of 1986, he moved to Atlanta, "for better economic opportunities." This was the beginning of the life Curtis had described.

"I was selling drugs on a pretty big volume. Close to the time I was busted, I was in a raid. They came shootin' through the door. I heard the first shot and just dropped. Dropped to the floor. I thought they were going to kill me; I thought they were going to kill us all. But we split, we scattered, and they never got to us. They robbed everyone of everything lying around. I had a gun, but it was locked in the car. I told the girl I was with to go get me the keys, but the keys had been stolen. I was going to kill them. I learned to shoot in the service. Right hand, left hand, I hit what I shoot.

"There were many times when I knew if someone tried to mess with me, I would kill him. They never did; but that's how out of control I was. I have never shot *anybody*, but I was prepared to kill.

"Then I was evicted; because I forgot to pay, or I didn't

bother, or because I was dealing drugs—I need to ask. I came
back to the apartment and found my belongings, my belongings
that was left, lying on the ground. I lost everything. *Everything*.
My photographs, my diplomas, my clothes. I had a full-length
beaver coat, and half-length fox." He laughed. "I dressed like a
drug dealer. I wore clothes that said 'drug dealer.' I drove a drug
dealer's car. If you had been around, and not run off to Africa,
you would have said, 'Why are you doing this?'

"On the night that I was caught—oh boy. OK. I picked up this
girl at four a.m. and her daughter—she worked as a stripper—
and took them home. I wasn't going to spend the night with her,
and I planned on seeing Twana. But Kimberly called, who I've
known a long time—before I met Benita—and she told me she
was pregnant. I said, 'Oh, no. Why did you go and do that? I already got a kid and it's more than I can handle.' She said, 'You
don't love me,' and we went back and forth, and hung up. And I
said, 'Forget it.' I was tired. I was tired. And I went to my car and
saw a young girl in the street, and called her over. She was a prostitute. And I said, 'Let's get together, and you give me some head.'

"That," said Billy evenly, for my information, "means 'oral
sex.' I should have known better. We went to one of the bad
ends of town, the drug ends, and then I said, let's go to a motel.'
And we were in the parking lot of the motel when the police
came. And I gave myself away. I said, 'I have a few ounces of
coke and some weed.' I gave myself away. And then they saw my
nine millimeter under the seat. I thought I had hidden it.

"So I was locked up for two weeks. I told Benita to get Twana
and take care of her. And I gave Lisa the money to manage. And
I got all four of them together on the phone at one time and told
them, 'You put aside your feminine differences, and work on
gettin' me out of here. Because I can't do anything from where I
am, but when I'm out, I can take care of business.' I gave the
money to Lisa—I couldn't lay that responsibility on Twana, and
Benita would have screwed it up. Kimberly still wasn't really
talking to me.

"I should have done a rehab program. I was pretty down at the time. I couldn't control my addiction. I was a drug addict. I was out for eight months, but the first thing I did after the lockup was get a weed. My lawyer let me down," he concluded elliptically, "and here I am."

As he made his way to the Coke machine, one of the guards strolled over to see how things were going.

"Billy is real positive," he said. "We could do with a lot more like him in here." (Had this been stage-managed?)

I had always known that Billy's background had been rough—or, as Billy said, "was street." Although his family was originally from the South, from Tuskegee, he had grown up in Cleveland, where his father still lived.

"My older brother, my big brother, he's a professional. All of a sudden, he just left. He used to brag about me; now I'm a criminal.

"I just wrote my dad a letter. My mom—you know, I always was basically alone. I've been more in touch with my family members now than I ever have been before. Because of this present incarceration. You know, I don't ax them for nothing, you know—I don't. They do the best they can, you know, I don't expect nothing—if anything, then it's a blessing—letters I get . . .

"I was adopted by my dad's sister. 'Cos my dad did some penal time; he did thirteen years. What for? That's, uh, personal. And I was adopted, you know. My mom, my biological mom, went to California. She had a choice between me and my oldest brother, and she chose to keep him. And her and my oldest brother, my sister, my other brother and other sister, were four. They went on to California, without me, and I was raised here, in Cleveland. I really was so young I—a lot had been told to me, so this is how I know what happened. I was under the assumption that the woman that raised me, who was really my aunt, was my legal adopted mom, until one day—I was thirteen—I was just coming back from playing, from bowling; I was with my family, and my dad—'cos I always had a relationship with him, because my mom would take me to prison to see him—he said, 'You know, your mom is coming back.' And I said, 'Man, what you telling me about my mom?' I said, 'No man, my mom is dead,' and he slapped me. And that's the first time he ever touched me, and the last time. And I went off the grid, man, because my dad was a big dude, and I was mad and crying. And his sister, which is his older sister, the one who raised me, she told him, 'What you doing, hitting my baby?' And she told him, she said to him, 'Boy, I raised *you*,' she said, 'but if you hit my son again, I will kill you.' And, see, she don't play; he knew that, he know it. They grew up in the South, and that old training is that my mom was the oldest and so she raised all the kids when her mom, my grandmom, had to go somewhere to work. She was the oldest, so she raised everybody. And he had that respect, and he was like, 'I'm sorry.' That helped, you know, to a point, where when I met my mom—my biological mom—and she asked me to go over there and meet them, and this and that, and my other brothers. And I met them, but, you know, thirteen years had elapsed, and you can only get a certain closeness.

"My mom that raised me—let me tell you, she was a blessed woman; she was strong, she was strong. She died. She passed in '87. A lot of me went with her when she passed. I was real . . . real bitter, and I really didn't care about life then. And when I had my oldest son, that helped bring me back to a little reality, sanity; but I still wasn't ready to handle the responsibilities of talking to others and helping. I was real self-centered, and I was still grieving.

"Do you want to know what the average day of my school day was like, my senior year? When I get up in the morning, Mom was—I was all on my own. I had a little nephew, he stayed with us, and most time, he would cook breakfast, 'cos I wouldn't cook. He was five years younger than me, but he could cook. After he cooked us breakfast, I go to high school. I report in for study hall. Me and about two other people, as soon as homeroom would start, we *bunked*. We *split*. We go out the door. We would just leave, literally, school until fourth period, which was about three hours later; we wouldn't be seen. We wouldn't go to no classes. And we go get drunk. We go get drunk and we gambled.

"Was there anything I liked in school? Sports! First of all, I wasn't—I didn't . . . See, my family didn't develop high—we didn't have study habits. You know, I passed and I didn't study. When it was time for a test, I took a test and passed. The hardest thing was Latin, because I didn't know Latin! Everything else came to me like nothing, so I didn't even study. And teachers was cool; they didn't press the issue. I'm sure it helped that I was an athlete, because if I wasn't doing nothing in this department, they probably would have kicked me out. I mean, I didn't get in a lot of trouble, but I was, you know, I was in a couple of fights. But I did come to school drunk sometimes. It was a trip.

"Our high school was ninety-nine out of a hundred. We had the ninety-ninth-worst academic record in the state of Ohio. High school. It was called Glenville High School. Glenville High School. Of *course* it would have made a difference if I would have had a teacher that was concerned enough, that if they seen that I wasn't coming to class would talk to my mother, would pursue to find out what's wrong with this individual; why don't he want to come to school? I mean, if I had someone that was of a teacher status to *show* concern, then it would have made a difference. I can't even remember a teacher's name. That I cared about. Other than the track teacher. I'm telling you, this is how vivid—I don't have . . . I don't have any memories. None! None!

"Let me tell you something; when I took my S.A.T., I didn't even know I had took a test and I had passed it, to be admitted into Florida State. I told that to Coach Bowden. I said, I don't even know if I took a SAT test. I said I don't even know if I can—if I'm able to even enter into your college. Enroll. And evidently, my scores was beyond it, was sufficient enough, and I didn't even know. Evidently it got me in. I had no concept of that.

"I'm telling you, I developed high self-esteem because of one reason. Because of the gift of my athletic ability. That . . . that helped me stimulate enough self-worth in myself to know that I'm *different*. I'm different. Athletically, I can do things. And then I started getting more self-esteem because I'm like, I can pass. I grasped things, and people liked me. People liked me.

"I played sports to keep me out of trouble, because I was always involved in gangs and violence. OK? Especially football, because I liked the *contact*. I was a small-frame person when I was growing up, and I liked physical contact, and it gave me a way to revert my aggressiveness out, you know, on people, without gettin' in trouble. And then I ran track because I was fast and competitive, you know, growin' up on the street, this was what we did. You know, on the streets we used to run against each other, and play football in the street, and tackle, and all of that stuff and that became a habit for me, and I liked it. So in school, that was acceptable, so I could do that.

"But it's many factors that happened in school—I . . . I . . . I used to get whupped, literally beaten. I was abused by a coach. Yeah man, he used to whup my legs with sticks. I'm telling him, 'Hold on, man, you know, I'm a little kid.' I know something wrong, but I couldn't really explain it, you know. I'm saying, 'Hold on. He ain't supposed to be beating on me because I'm trying to punt a ball, and I had never been a punter in my life— I ain't got no background for that. I've always been a running back, or a wide receiver. I'm trying to do this for the team, and I'm gettin' beat for this?' Man, it got ugly for me; it distorted my whole perception for being a kid and enjoying the sport I enjoyed. He used to tear me up. I ain't even focused on nobody else, all I know is"—Billy laughed—"he used to tear *me* up. I be like—my thighs be swollen. Other teachers, they didn't say nothing; that's what I'm trying to say—this was socially acceptable. This abnormal behavior, it was acceptable. That's just like if you been raised in an alcoholic family all your life, you don't know no better; you think this is how it's supposed to be—this is family

life. And it's destructive, it's dysfunctional, whoever the alcoholic is, but you don't know no better, so you think it's normal;
and it's ab-normal. Man, I was through. I gave up, because I said,
'Hey, man, if sports is taking people, hitting them, hittin' me—
especially a game that I loved, football??? I can't handle this.
You know, I ain't going to be beaten.' And then we were having
a losing season, and I'm like, man, forget this. And that's what
made me join the service.

"I first went towards the marines, but I had a brother in there
and he told me 'Don't go to the marines, man, don't you come to
this marines.' He said, 'This ain't no place for you, 'cos I'm getting out of here as soon as my time get done.' I had signed the paperwork to get into the marines, and I had to go back in there
and tell them that I'm going to the air force. I had an uncle in the
air force. I knew I got to learn responsibility and life. Yeah, because I wanted to live to be a man, and I knew that I wasn't going
to be a man and survive the streets of Cleveland. 'Cos all my
friends, they was in gangs—I was wild.

"I was sent to Lackland Air Force Base, San Antonio, Texas.
I'm a seventeen-year-old boy, now, you know just left home—
straight—and I'm out here with all these folks. We didn't have
no forced integration thing, with us, we at Glenville—it wasn't
about that. Blacks stayed at one side, whites on another. Whites
on the west side; blacks on the east. This is how it was. This stuff
started getting forced after '76, when I graduated from high
school, so I didn't have no relationship—you following me?—
none, with the whites, *any* other. Mexican? None of that! All I
knew was how blacks mixed. You know, we had white teachers,
but I didn't have no relationships with no teachers; I had no reason—I didn't go to class.

"Once I graduated from the boot camp program, I went to
flight school, and from there I became—what you call—they
elect me flight leader, that's in charge of my whole flight. Then
they had an election to be in charge of the squadron; you have six
flights, and that's one squadron, and I ended up being the

squadron leader. I was just going on eighteen; I turned eighteen in September, and I had all of this responsibility. I was in charge of all this—it was good for me. It helped develop my teamworkship, and officers, you know, they liked me. I had one officer who used to always tell me, he said, 'Billy, once you learn the universal language you going to be more successful in life'; 'cos I used to talk street—slang—that's how I grew up.

"You know it took me—as I was coming into Florida State, I was developing it, that's when I started using it. You know—I'm going to tell you something; believe it or not, the first couple of months at Florida State was the most critical time as far as me saying I can make it or not. Yeah. Because I had a fear factor. The fear factor. It's called poverty. Not wanting to return. Not just economic poverty. Illiterate poverty. Generation on generation of negative thinking. You are scared to fail, so you stay right where you are. I might have didn't act like it, but shoot, I was scared to death. 'Cos I ain't had no training; and then you hear about my background and high school, so I'm like—and you played a great part. When you left it hurt me a little bit; it *helped* me because I was dependent on you, 'cos you gave me a confidence within myself. When you left, I didn't have anyone who *knew* me. The only thing they knew about me was what they could see. The athlete. The physical specimen. I was a piece of meat. You always believed more in me than I did in myself, academically."

From the outside, the buildings, although attractive in their way, looked vaguely derelict. I had caught sight of one or two upper-story porches in which inmates were lounging around, but even here, in the relative open, things looked cramped and sordid. Yet Billy himself seemed so well and—in his words—"positive," that I wondered if life inside was more amenable than it appeared. In particular, I wondered how he passed his time. I assumed that, as in a summer camp, virtually every hour was blocked out with some kind of activity, so as to keep people occupied and out of trouble. Apparently this was not the case.

"Oh no. No, no, no, no. Naw. There's no . . . no. No. The administration—no. No activities, no. See, their main policy and concept is to make sure that they have a certain number of people returning. Eighty percent of the general population return. Of course they want that! This is a money industry." He laughed. "They don't care about rehabilitation. Oh, come on. Yes, I'm serious—eighty percent of the people come back here. It's a hotel. That's exactly what it is. Room and board. They charge the state room and board. Yes sir. They get paid for this. This is nothing but a money scam. They don't stress no rehabilitation, they just pass some low law saying that those that try to help themselves will get a certain limited time cut off their prison sentence, but that ain't nothing but a money scam trip. But that's why what I'm trying to do—if this program can get into effect, it's gonna allow prisoners to realize that they doing this for themselves; the institution ain't doing this. They can stay out and make a difference and develop an outreach program; all the positive things you do, you can put it into, like, a résumé, and send it out to various outreach programs, who can assist you in finding work, so that when you get out of here, you're already established. And you can make a positive contribution into society. Let me tell you something; since I been locked down since August of '91, the best counselor I ever had is the counselor I got right now, and it's just been a blessing, because she is the only one who will do the functions a counselor is supposed to do. You know, this . . . this— they don't stress nothing like this here.

"The general population here is very violent and very negative, you know, very disrespectful—low self-worth, self-esteem. People sometimes fighting, but when I see it, I stop it. It's stupid. Me? Me?! Girl, who's going to beat on *me*?" He laughed holding his arms out wide.

"But some, they act like animals, the majority of them, like they have no home training. Like they just desire to continue to live a very destructive life, and really don't care about nobody else."

("They come from all levels," Billy's counselor had told me, in her hard, no-nonsense, seen-it-all Georgia voice. "Those in our instructional program tend to have better training; the others don't have the IQs. Some are indigent and illiterate; they come from alcoholic families where the parents didn't know if they were in school or not.")

"But there are still a few in the general population that do desire a change, and want to change, but don't know how to; it's just routine. People live by the pattern that they've lived for years, you know, they just following other misguided people, because nobody stepping out there and saying, 'Hey man, you can make a difference in your life, and this is how you do it.' This program—what we do is offer them that alternative. This is what this program gonna do.

"A lot of people don't know that faith overcome fear. People think that having faith is just believing in a higher power, but that's the start; faith is being an active thinker, is eliminating and weighing consequences, and taking the right actions. It takes just a little common sense. And if you can apply it, then what you will do, you will find out that the problem is not as serious as you once thought or once conceived. I know this now, and I believe this, and even in here, I strive—positive thoughts, keeping a positive-mental-attitude. *This* is my foundation. See, most people want to start their foundation once they get out, you know— 'When I get out, I'm gonna do this, I'm gonna do that.' But I feel that you need to first enhance yourself and change your thinking inside here, and once you do it here, you can develop to see a brighter future, because you got a foundation to start upon. Because once you get out, you have so many distractions that if you ain't learned to be focused and disciplined in here, you in trouble. And I know that. I have friends that been out and been back. And the point is, *I* been out there, and I know how it is not to be disciplined, not to have a focus point—you followin' me? I'm not going—no, I did that for thirty-something years, and in between I had highlights, you know, very blessed periods in my life where I done things and contributed to life, but I have also had very low points where I was destructive and detrimental to myself and others around me and I took it, saying 'This is life,' and I just shook it off. And that's bull, and that ain't how life is meant to be; that's how I *chose* how *my* life to be. But now, I'm going nowhere but positive, and I am going to take seriously that I am my brother's keeper.

"When I get out, I'm going to go around and I'm going to be, hopefully, giving testimonies, speaking to churches and schools and hopefully can develop from schools and go on to colleges. And I'll speak on various aspects, especially definitely how, you know, I changed my thought patterns with the grace of God to get into positive mental thinking, developing a purpose in life, utilizing my time more productively. I think it's going to happen like that—I mean as soon as I give my first testimony. Because I really think that when people do things that are positive, what will happen is that other people will cooperate around them, will give them opportunities. If you doing what you supposed to be doing, when opportunities knock, then you can take advantage.

"You know, what I'm in the process of doing here—there is a director, an executive director, and program director and I'm going to get in touch with them, and try the New Christian Men for Life. It's a drug and rehabilitation program that I'm trying to get into. If things work out right, they have programs where you give testimony on your life; it's a six- to nine-month program, halfway house program, that will give me the opportunity to glorify God and also allow—and, yeah, that's it. Just glorify God, because then everything else is going to happen. I mean, I know that. My life speaks for itself; and I know that it's a purpose for everything that has happened, and as I confess and I say all these things, I also going to allow people to realize that they can change their own destiny. You know, I'm going to give people self-hope."

I muttered something about learning specific skills, about solid education being of more practical importance. Billy looked hard at me.

"What do you think I been saying? What? *Before* education, it is their attitude . . . I want them, kids, to think, for the first time. I want them to look at reality for the first time. Your thought patterns control your destiny. They've heard 'Get a job, get an education.' What does that—they don't know what that *means*, feeling as they feel. I want them to know. . . ." He floundered for a moment, exasperated, groping for the words. "I want them to know that even when they do negative things—they are in control. They *chose* to do those things. They *are* controlling their own destiny. Every negative action, they have a choice; they can do it, or they can walk away. If they do it, that's a choice. But that same power to choose, that same choice, could be used for the positive. To enhance their own lives.

"Even in this *nnnnegative* environment, it has been a positive blessing for me, because it gave me an opportunity to see me, for the first time, me. *Me.* I wake up, I look at me, you know, I . . . I . . . I spend time—quiet time, silent time—with me. Me and God. We all have capabilities, the thing is how to get to those capabilities, how to get to that thought pattern. How to apply the faith, how to motivate and . . . and . . . and withdraw that energy, that untapped power that's there for you, you understand?"

"But Billy, Billy, Billy," I interrupted. The voice of Napoleon Hill tangled up in Billy's own words had become unbearable to me. "But Billy, see—what I feel is that you always knew that."

"Ohhhh, sweetheart. I did to a certain degree."

"But Billy, look at it. You're serving time now, but, you know—the odds were you should have been killed on the streets; the odds were you should have been in juvenile detention in high school; the odds were you shouldn't have graduated from high school; the odds were that once you graduated, then you really should have bust loose and got in trouble; the odds . . . the odds for you going to Florida State—joining the service and graduat-

ing from that, going to Florida State, getting a football scholarship—the odds were thousands to none, and you beat the odds."
    "Caroline. Listen to what I'm saying. Even in the service, I was
in black marketing. I was doing things that no one should be
doing. I wouldn't even go to work. I was AWOL. But because of
my athletic ability, they overlooked it. You . . . you . . . you—I
mean, I was still, I still had very negative thought patterns, and I
was living a destructive life; but a lot of positive things was happening in my life that overshadowed the negative things so I was
gettin' away with *murder*. That's what was happening. And it's
got to a point where now I have no choice but to go back and
reface them fears; and the thoughts and the memories come up
and now I find out, 'Oh so this is what was going on.' Because
I'm realizing certain barriers. In this program, I can realize, 'Oh
this is me. This is why I did what I did.' Because the man—
my father that raised me, see, my father that raised me was an
alcoholic.
    "There's many out there that might be, quote, what society
calls successful and really is not. Truly, deep inside, he is just as
confused and life is unmanageable as ever. You following me?
Society might think how blessed your life is, in actuality it's a
curse, it's a nightmare, because you don't have any inner peace.
Man, I . . . I—there used to be times, man, I used to go *crazy*.
You think I was around there, thinking anything cool? It wasn't
cool. Nothing was right for me. I wasn't really doing what I
wanted to do. But I didn't know what I wanted to do. Thirty-
three years. I was doing that. Thirty-three years. Doing whatever
I wanted to do. It's a blessing that I never was to a point where I
had the mentality where I was trying to hurt people, allowed my
addiction to control to a point where it was violent. Do you follow what I mean? Yeah, well I never got to that point. But I knew
that I wasn't doing—I knew that my life was supposed to be
doing something to help others and I didn't know how to tap
that, to get to it. I wasn't balanced.
    "I talked with my father. He told me do something construc-

tive with life while I'm in here. I came in here with the attitude
that I ain't going to socialize. I came in here for myself. Someone
does something to me, I'm gonna do it to them. I even ran a store
here. Charge one and one-half over. Thirty dollars a month on
the books. I was gonna hurt people. That was acceptable.

"Every time I tried to change, I thought the system was stopping me. Every time I had an obstacle, I blamed it—the system.
But I started breakin' up fights. I started thinking of the Islamic
faith, but it didn't feel right for me. I started lookin' into Chris-
tianity. My four-year-old son asked me, 'Do you know who Jesus
is?' I couldn't answer him. He wasn't *my* savior. I knew him as a
prophet. December twenty-fifth, 1992, was a spiritual awakening
for me. It made me realize that I needed to allow God to help me
control my life. He placed me in a situation where I can learn to
help others, learn to help me.

"Now, I call this a good experience. Because this is a time of
healing and growing for me and developing, you know, and this
is a place where—look! Look! I'm talking to you. Think about it;
if I'd have been out there—no telling; you probably wouldn't
have never been able to reach me, because I didn't have a phone;
I wasn't listed. And my lifestyle definitely wasn't conducive to a
point where anyone could reach me—I kept it that way. And I
started drifting away from a lot of friends. But I'm gettin' it
again—eye of the tiger! I'm hungry; I'm focused. I feel better
now, Caroline, than I have in years."

Billy was in regular contact with his son who lived in Atlanta.
Of his son by his child bride in New York, he had no knowledge,
other than that he was being taken care of by public assistance.
The son in Atlanta evidently already showed signs of being an
athlete, but Billy did not want his head turned by too much talk
of his abilities.

"I want him to think of himself as more than an athlete.

"No, I am not worried that my son come here, and see his dad
in prison. *I* am not in prison because my father served time. I am
in prison because at a certain point in my life, I decided to make

money selling drugs. We all defined to some extent by our social circumstances. But not entirely defined. We have something here," tapping his head. "I knew that there were certain obstacles I would have to overcome. It starts early. Earlier than college, earlier than high school. In the family. But you do not say to your kid, 'Because this is where you from, you gonna fail.'

"I have often thought that the people who say those kinds of things, that we are victims of the system, of society, *minority* spokesmen, are so smart that they don't understand what the people below them are like. They believe that everybody would be like them and that the government is all that stop them. The government don't stop nobody. Not now. We're through those times. We all learned that history. We're talking about people who can't take responsibility for themselves.

"My son, I want him to learn. But basically, the values of our system is not based on education. Oh come on. Look around you. There are no evident rewards. Our society, they *want* us illiterate. It's just a form of indentured servitude. Kids are not *forced* to enhance themselves educationally. They are not *forced* to learn basic skills. It should be *forced* upon us. We, as kids, should not have the freedom of choice to learn.

"A college degree is necessary because society finds it desirable; they feel better for them knowing that everybody has this experience. And it makes economic sense. It's sad to say that our educational system is a business—not a real lucrative business, but a business. But there should be some technical training; Fortune 500 should have a say in the curriculum, not just the teachers.

"Education is valueless to the young, because they already feel they don't need it. If I feel I can't learn—I will look for other means. I will find a world where I will be acceptable. As a drug dealer, as a prostitute. There *are* people who look up to these.

"And what are *you* going to do? What are your dreams?" Billy asked suddenly, shifting the focus and looking hard at me.

"Mine? I suppose writing. Writing a good book. Writing one good book."

"Writing is one-dimensional. What else?"

"Well . . . well—I'm looking. I don't seem to have a burning desire for anything anymore."

"I don't know what it is about you, Caroline; you not *bored*, but you definitely not fulfilled. Writing this book is not going to fill that void. Find something useful. Get busy, baby."

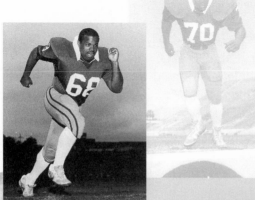

LENNY

My most abiding memory of Lenny Chavers is of him standing on the steps of the Strozier Library one spring day, peering around to the right and left, naked anxiety suffusing his broad face, on the lookout for me. I had received an emergency phone call from him, something that no one else had ever ventured to make, and had agreed to meet him, as I was going to be on campus anyway. Catching sight of me as I walked under the big live oak that stands just outside the library, he waved his arms and met me halfway down the steps in great agitation.

"I got the books inside," he said, and headed through the library doors, bumping into people and talking over his shoulder as he made his way to a desk in the reference section that was piled almost to the height of my head with encyclopedias and dictionaries and general books about music, all open to pages headed with the word "Jazz." It seemed that Lenny, who had an easy liking for Grover Washington Jr., had committed himself to writing a paper on this particular genre for his music class, assuming it would be something that he could whip off without much trouble. To his amazement and dismay, it was now revealed to him that whole books had in fact been written on this topic and that even the encyclopedic entries ran to many pages of small print. Settled hopelessly amid his books, he reminded me of the princess in the old fairy tale who has been given the cruel task of sorting an immense pile of mingled grains into separate bags of barley, rice, and wheat. The deadline for Lenny's task, as for the princess's, was the following morning.

"How he expect me to read all these books by tomorrow?" said Lenny, panic now having given way to indignation. Judging that the most constructive tack at this juncture was to get the paper under way, I did not point out that the assignment was several weeks old, but explained instead that the instructor wouldn't expect a book-length paper from Lenny, nor for him to have read every work written on the subject. We discussed possible outlines and strategies, and shortly afterward I left him, woebegone but calm, hidden behind his barricade of books.

That same evening at study hall, it was the old sunny, jolly, beaming Lenny Chavers who turned up, his work done, not a care in the world. Casually, he gave me his paper to look at, and I read it until I came to the following: "One of the giants of jazz of this period, as indeed of all periods, was Louis Armstrong, who delighted audiences with his inspired horn playing and his warm, puff voice." Calling Lenny over, I drew his attention to the final phrase, asking him what he thought it meant. Ever obliging and cooperative, he good-naturedly read it through in silence, then looked up, genuinely baffled.

"I think you miswrote 'puff' for 'gruff' when you copied this whole paper word for word out of the encyclopedia."

Lenny's face did not drop; in fact his look of puzzlement lifted—of course, that was what exactly what had happened! Now it was all clear.

"Gaawwwleee," he said, taking his paper and turning to the other players. "Caroline didn't take but one look at my paper and she know right away I cheated." Lenny was impressed, and as a bonus the incident had given him yet another story to tell. Lenny had realized early on that most events eventually make good stories, and thus life presented him with endlessly amusing anecdotal possibilities.

Lenny's physical features appeared to have been specifically fashioned to accommodate his laughter. His face was large and round and always in expressive, excited motion, his smile enormous. Although big, he was contoured like the Michelin tire man, or the Pillsbury Doughboy, and I could not imagine anyone being intimidated by his size. His thighs were so big that they rubbed conspicuously together as he walked, and when the other players caught sight of him approaching, they would call out in unison "Ow, ouch, ow, ouch" as the two big thighs rubbed against each other. Lenny himself always found this enormously funny and on reaching them would have to collapse in laughter into a chair in order to recover.

I cannot recall ever witnessing a situation from which he did not eventually emerge in good spirits. There were bad grades; there were bad practices, bad games, bad moments which he responded to with despondency—but as soon as he had found an opportunity to tell about the event, in the very process of the telling his fancy snagged on the inevitable nugget of humor, and he concluded by making himself and usually anyone listening begin to laugh. He would go over and over an event or a description, repeating it until he had exhausted its comic potential, and then turn to something else. He was never malicious, and part of what made him so immensely likable was the unmistakable good-heartedness that brimmed out in his laughter.

There was also something eminently sensible about his outlook, which manifested itself in small details: he drove a bright orange VW Beetle, a modest and unflashy car that few of the other players would have deigned to choose. He had determined his major—criminology—early on and had a clear idea of what he could do with the degree; several of his relatives were in this field and he seemed to use them as concrete examples of what was possible in life, rather than only dreaming of the pros.

From his written work, I judged that while there were significant gaps in his knowledge of basic grammar, he had a fighting chance and was not, on the whole, completely in over his head, although he himself must have thought at times that he was.

"How can they expect us black people to learn English?" he asked in frustration one night when the whole class was sitting around the table in the study room, doing exercises out of their workbooks. And it was Lenny who on the first day of our class had asked me worriedly, "Didn't they tell you? We ain't *got* no grammar."

"Well the first thing you should know about big Lenny is that there's a lot less of him." I was talking to Detective Gaylon White, a former F.S.U. player and colleague of Lenny's at the Florida Department of Law Enforcement, where Lenny had worked after graduation from Florida State. To my astonishment, I learned that Lenny had become a passionate devotee of bodybuilding, and his former jovially rotund outline had been streamlined into hard contours.

"You could have passed him in the hall and not known who he was," Detective White said.

Lenny had left the department a few years ago and gone to Tampa with a friend to run a gym. Detective White didn't have his telephone number, but I obtained that of his parents' home, farther south in Florida.

Mrs. Chavers welcomed a chance to talk about her son and told me that Lenny was married, that he had left the gym and was working two jobs, and that he and his wife had just had their first baby.

"I wanted to go down and see the baby when she was born, but Lenny said she was too young to have visitors—he knew I would bring down all my grandchildren and he wants to give the baby time before she faces a crowd."

"So Lenny knows all about being a father." I laughed. A picture of him had flashed in my mind's eye, as I had seen him on the library steps, waving his arms in agitation—"Back, back, you-all get back. . . ."

"Oh yes," said Mrs. Chavers. "He took a course. He came down on Mother's Day, though, and took me to his home. It was the best present he could have given me. I wish they had all turned out like Lenny," Mrs. Chavers said, in her sweet, thoughtful southern voice. "I sure am proud of him. I just hope—I just hope he stays this way. There are so many . . . temptations in this world."

Mrs. Chavers gave me Lenny's telephone number and took mine just in case he called.

"Your name is C-a-r-o-l-i-n-e, Caroline? And you tutored him in 1981? T-u-t-o-r-e-d, tutored. I'll let him know if he calls."

I had arranged to meet Lenny at a designated place at the Tampa airport, and I was standing alone waiting when a red Honda with smoky windows pulled up, through the dark glass of which I could just discern the outline of a massive, square-topped head. The window rolled down slowly, revealing the Terminator for the top few inches, and Lenny Chavers under that, his hair clipped up into a formidable flat high-top. He was, I judged, and as he later told me, somewhere between his old football weight and his peak bodybuilding ideal, although his chest and arms were balloonlike, so inflated that they looked, quite literally, as if they had been pumped full of helium.

"Yes, I recognize you now," he said, helping me into the car. Lenny had grown a little mustache, but it was rendered so insignificant by the sheer size of his smile as to be almost invisible. When we had last spoken on the phone, Lenny had been in the process of applying for a new job, as a parole officer. He had been optimistic about his prospects, as the interview had gone extremely well and all of his references and background information had been checked out, usually a sure sign that an offer is imminent. As we drove toward his home, I asked him if he had got the job, and in answer he launched into an amazing story: No, he had not got the job, but had been told by a well-intentioned insider that he should check out his record with the Florida Department of Law Enforcement in Tallahassee, where he had worked before coming to Tampa. He did so, taking a day off to drive to Talla-hassee, and was shaken to discover that a former supervisor had written that he would under no circumstances hire Lenny Chavers again.

"My mouth was hanging open. I couldn't believe it. I mean, I thought I'd left on good terms—I had been using them as a reference. This man had a list of things I had done—insubordination pending; falsification of records; disregard for regulations. I was shocked. But when I read the report you know, I—'falsification': I had been been imprinting fingerprints and at the end of the day you have to add them all up, how many you've done. I wrote like one hundred ninety-eight, one hundred ninety-nine, and I had done two hundred. 'Insubordination': I took a day of leave for the delivery of my baby—I requested written permission but I couldn't find the specific person immediately over me to sign it, so someone higher did. I'm trying to straighten it out. My immediate supervisor, he's the one I had the one-on-one contact with, and he's the one that wrote that down. I need to deal with *that*, that's what I need to do—and he's no longer there. That's what I'm running up against, he's no longer there, and there are other people there I can talk to, but I haven't gotten round to talking to people yet, because every time I call up there, they're either not there, or they left for the day—that's why I had to go up to Tallahassee myself. I got my records and everything, you know, and I'm working on it now. You know, and I've been wondering why for two years I couldn't get a job in law enforcement. I knew I always came close, you know, I knew I was doing well in the interviews and everything—so now I know why. Until I get this straightened out—I may as well throw my degree away," he said, but his voice was already bubbling into laughter. "Just throw it away; just throw it down the toilet," and then came the big belly laugh, as of old.

Tampa itself I never saw. We skirted the airport, passing a few housing estates that had been planted on the chessboard-flat land, arriving eventually in an area that looked only newly domesticated. A surviving scattering of stately moss-hung live oak trees still cast their centuries' old shade along the road, leading the way to the hastily thrown up apartment houses. Here we parked, and Lenny led the way around the corner of a short dark passageway to a door that opened on his domicile: a small living room that tapered to a dining area large enough to contain a table and four chairs, a kitchen alcove, and beyond this, as I surmised, the bedroom.

Lenny's wife, Marinette, came in holding the baby, while Lenny looked on proudly, still in awe of this extraordinary event in his life. Marinette was a tall, graceful, strikingly pretty woman, with a long elegant face and slanting, almost Oriental eyes, the same eyes that could be seen in the sleepy, screwed-up face of Alexis Ashley Chavers. A few minutes later, Marinette's mother, who lived only half an hour away, flew into the apartment, swooping up her daughter and the baby. The two women disappeared into the bedroom and could be heard laughing and cooing and singing with Alexis.

Lenny settled his bulging frame onto one of the living room's two sofas, facing a gigantic television screen that was turned on, with the sound down, to a sports station.

"Yes, I'm a proud father now. It's like it changes everything."

Lenny worked, as his mother had said, two jobs: during the day as a court officer and at night as a security guard for a local store. Leaving early in the morning, he didn't get home most days until half past nine at night.

"Right now, I work in the court. The other guys get so mad when people say, 'Hey, security guard!' Those guys get so mad." His laugh was already working its way up, as he warmed to the tale. "Because we have guys, ex–police officers, guys that, you know, they've been police officers but they've retired and they get this job and it makes them so mad—'Hey, guard!' you know. They're like, 'We are not *guards*.' They actually are guards, but they just don't want to be recognized as being a guard, you know, it sound like," he growled, " *'Guard!'*

"We had a big fight two days ago; you know this guy tried to run out—he was having a court hearing and he violated his probation; it was a sixteen-year-old guy, and he violated his probation. I don't know what got into him, but he just thought he was going to run out of the courthouse, just run—he just took off running. So we had to catch him. This guy, he just violated his probation, but now he's a sixteen-year-old guy and he's going to be tried for escape. So that's another ten years. And that's all he did, violate probation. I mean, I guess he just panicked, I don't know what they think of. I just don't know. I don't know what cross people's minds when they want to just run—where can they go? You got police officers coming in and out and you got security and you got bailiffs, and all this law enforcement and he thinks he's going to get out of that courthouse. If he wouldn't have tried to escape, he probably would have been out in another two months. He's not going to get community control or nothing; he's not going to get work release or nothing, because they're going to think he's going to run. He's going to do his time, straight time. He's not going to get no parole or nothing. And he's only sixteen.

"I was an input technician in Tallahassee, and I got so—I just got tired of sitting down at that desk, and it was an entry-level job anyway, it wasn't anything real significant, you know, and that's why I got into bodybuilding, I just got so tired of sitting down. So what I did, I got into bodybuilding, and my body just *took* off, you understand—I had found my niche. You know, I have been lifting weights since high school. I went from two hundred and eighty pounds to one hundred ninety-five in a year. People didn't recognize me; they thought I was someone else. I went to a game in Tallahassee and someone came up and asked me did I have a brother called Lenny who once played for F.S.U. I was working out an hour and a half in the morning and an hour and a half in the evening and I entered the Mr. Tallahassee competition—people said I looked good. I went through to the finals, but lost in the finals. But I had found something there—I thought I had found my niche. So I said to myself, why not work at a gym or something and then try to get onto the police force? So that's what I did. I left F.D.L.E. and I came and I worked at Balley's, which is a gym. And I was working out there, and I tried to get onto Tampa, St. Pete, police, and I couldn't get on—and now I know why; now I know. Someone advised me to apply elsewhere, you know, not in Tampa itself, and that's what I did. I applied in Polk County which is about twenty miles away from here, thirty miles away from, and I went on to interview last week for a position, and I told the man who interviewed me that I had something come up on my background. He said we usually look at the job that you have now, that's what we concentrate on, we don't usually look back that far—we do, but, you know, we don't take that into consideration, not as much as the job where you at now. So I felt sort of good about that. And I warned him. But here in Tampa, see, they look at that, because they want to find something that drop you down, because you have so *many* applicants that if they find something that can knock you down, they go for that.

"My brother is in a criminology career—he's actually a probation officer. I got an uncle—he's in the criminology field. He went to Bethune Cookman. He graduated in criminology and he's working at a prison down in Belle Glade, so that's what sort of got me interested in the criminology field; and I figured it would be a good thing because, you know, the place where I'm from there was so much negativity there—you know, drugs, that kind of place, you know—I felt that was a good thing for me to do, get in that field. I like helping people.

"The neighborhood where I grew up, you know—drugs, you know how peer pressure is, you want to—but I think I was strong enough to get out of that. And one of the things that helped me was sports; sports really helped me get out of that atmosphere, you know, of being negative, because I sort of isolated myself from the other people. When I see other people doing wrong, I sort of went the other way. There was always something that kept me from going that way; I don't know why. I just wanted to do good. I always wanted to do the right thing, you know, and I thought drugs was the wrong thing to do. I never felt comfortable when I went with them to do whatever they want to do, I never felt comfortable, I always felt it was wrong. You know—'Why, why am I doing this?' That's why I always went the other way. And so I think that helped me, because my brother, I think—my brother was the best athlete in my family. I mean, I had older brothers that went to college and played football, you know, great athletes, but my brother, this brother, he was like the ideal height, six-foot-two, he was smart, I mean he was smart, he was really intelligent, and he just turned that other thing, he turned to drugs. I think it's peer pressure, I think it's—that's what I really think it is. I think you see friends, some people that you meet, that you run into, that say, 'Hey, let's do this,' and you do it. And they say 'There's nothing really wrong with it,' and you keep doing it, and you keep doing it, and all of a sudden you're trapped. You can't leave. And you look back and you're like—'God.' My mom always tell me—my mom who you talked to?—'Frank always wanted to follow you. If he would have just went your direction'—because I always went the other way. When they went this way, I went that way. Because I knew it was *wrong*. And you know, she said, 'Frank always wanted to follow you,' but now he's . . . he's doing bad. And he was the *best* athlete—that's what my father said. He was the best athlete in the family. I had five brothers, all athletic. My oldest brother, he got a scholarship to F.A.M.U. to play—wrestling, everything, he was so talented. My next-to-oldest brother, he went to school, you know, he went to school, he went to school on a scholarship, he didn't go on a sports scholarship—but he was athletic also. Frank was behind him, and he was—he had it all. He was well rounded. I mean, he had people looking at him in eighth grade because he was so tall, and they was just looking at him. And he was the best athlete. What does he do now? Sshhh. Nothing. He doesn't do anything. He's thirty-three. In fact, he's in jail now.

"Why do they do it? People have been trying to answer that question for so long. People think it's—a lot of people think it's parents, but I don't . . . I don't think it's parents. A lot of people do; I mean they say, 'Well, parents have that responsibility to show them, to tell them to do the right things, and they should try to instill that, and if they don't do it, they should punish them, and they should keep trying to discipline them to do the right thing.' But, it goes to show you—like *me*. I mean, I went this way, and my brother went that way, and we were raised by the same parents. That's why I try to tell my parents, I mean, because we got three that went one way, and three that went the other way. Parents have a lot to do with it also, but I really think it's the person too. It's the person; there comes a time in your life when you have to make a decision, and if you make that wrong decision, that's you. That's not a parent. And once you get to that age where you can make that decision, then you got to suffer the consequences, whether it's good or bad. It's the person.

"I was recruited by several schools, I visited several schools. They have certain boosters that are in the area and they visit your house. I had several people visit my house. Coach Bowden never come to my house, but they have assistant coaches that come to your house, visit your parents, talk to your parents. One of the reasons why I chose F.S.U. was because I knew the area, and I could just go anywhere I pleased, because I had relatives that were there also. I had cousins that lived in Havana, twenty, thirty minutes away, so I had a place to go.

"My first impression was that Tallahassee was big. A lot of students. That was my first impression. But it really wasn't a college atmosphere for us, if you were an athlete, because we got everything taken care of. We really didn't go get our books, we really didn't fit in with the people. You know, you're a football player. You're not really a student—that's how they look at you. That's what they think of you. It wasn't really a college atmosphere until I went to summer school; that's when it was like you feel like a student, you know, you're hanging around that student union.

The rest of the time you really weren't a student per se, you were an athlete-student—that's what it really is.

"The only thing that intimidated me a little was the size, the size of the class. You look around, you have five hundred students, you know—wait a minute now! It's like—how can this guy know that you're in school? In high school they call your name, they say if you are here. It's like, how they going to know? You don't have to go into class. You see some people that you only see during the tests. You're like—'*You're* in my class, man?!'

"When I first went to F.S.U. from high school, I didn't know I was going to get a degree, because like any other person that goes to F.S.U. on a scholarship, they think they're going to go to pros. I was All-State in football, All-State in everything; I had the body, I was bench-press champion in high school, all this— I didn't have any time to play it all, so I only chose wrestling, weight lifting, and football, because I felt, you know, basketball wouldn't have helped me in becoming a better football player, you know, and all the things I did was around football. Like wrestling helped me become a better football player because of that agility and moving. Weight lifting got me stronger in order to play football. So it was always geared around football. I knew I was going to go to college. I knew it. I don't know why—I guess I had two brothers in school. But really, to be honest with you, it really wasn't my number-one priority was to get a degree. It wasn't. My number-one priority was to play football. They sort of tell you that—I mean they don't really tell you, but it's instilled in you, saying—they say that, 'Hey, you wouldn't be in school without football.' And it's really true; you wouldn't. You wouldn't really be there if it wasn't for that football scholarship, so they don't come out and tell you football is number one, and the school is number two, but you see that it is. Football is number *one* on their list, and you try to change *their* mind. You know, you try to go to class, you try to do all the right things, so they say, 'Hey, this guy's really into school,' so they sort of let you go your way. If you helping them out on the football field, they're all right about it, because they see that you're a well-rounded guy—you doing good in school and you're helping them out in football; but if they see it going one way or the other, you know, they want it to go this way, to football. They really don't care about the other way, that's up to you. So, you can't blame them, because that's their jobs, that's what they get paid for. It's business, that's what it is, and it's money.

"And all these guys that are up here, they're making money, they're making so *much* money—and I don't understand why they don't get paid, the football players here, in college—they should get paid, they should get something. I mean, granted, that people say—people that just go to school—say, 'Gaaww, what do you want? You getting your class paid for, you getting your books paid for, you getting your food—you getting everything paid for. Why you want some more money?' But they're making so much money off you, and you can't just live off that. You just can't. And you got to know, forty percent of these athletes that go to class, they don't come from a background where you can just call your parents—'Hey, I need a hundred dollars,' and they say 'Hey, here you go.' They come from a background that's not that good. You know, it's—I mean I come from a background that was all right, I mean, I guess we were so close, our family, that we didn't look at that we were in poverty or anything; we weren't in poverty, but we weren't well off. We had to work, my father had to work in order to provide for us, and that's what he did; he worked and he worked and he tried to be at the games you know, he used to drive trucks. He doesn't do it anymore, he's retired now. My mother had jobs, odds and ends jobs, she used to work at a factory, this glass company, she worked at a factory there for a long time. They don't work anymore and they want to enjoy themselves now, but they can't. Because they got grandchildren and my *brother*. You know, his kids are there with them.

"In high school, I think it was, you know, you're sort of brainwashed when you're in high school; that's the way I was. I was so into football, so into athletics; I mean, it's sort of they were holding you, pushing you along, because of being an athlete. And I think, and you never notice this in high school, but you are—you were helped along because you were an athlete; you helped the school, so they're going to in essence help you. I could've been an above-average student. I could have, because this lady—she was my tutor in high school, and her name was Carol Halls, and I used to go over there and she used to help me out in school. She'd say, 'Gaaww, if you'd study a little harder, you'd be so intelligent, I mean you get this stuff so easy, but you just don't want to do it.' And she was right, I just didn't want to take the time— because I felt that I didn't have to. I just wanted to pass in order to play football. That was my mentality back then; I wanted to do it in order to play football.

"School was not my number-one priority, until I was like, until I got my leg broke, my second year at F.S.U. 'Eighty-two, 'eighty-three. That's when I realized, now you buckle down, now you need to buckle down to school. I had pulled ligaments—it wasn't broken or anything, I had a operation on it, I had arthroscopic surgery; it was a little poke of a scope. That was when I realized that football isn't everything. I played after that, I was playing, but it was never the same. This wasn't number one. Football is something secondary. I didn't want to quit; once I start something, I'm going to do it, and in school I always say— 'Hey, I come here to graduate, I'm going to do it.'

"Nothing whatsoever stayed with me from school. Because I was telling this guy, this Roy guy, who I work with—he's going to school now. He's like, 'You got your degree right?' I was like, 'Yes.' He's like, 'Gaaw, what is this? Psychology?' I was like, 'Man! That's been sooo long.' I was like—'I'm going to go back to school. I'm going to go back to school'; if you don't use it, you lose it. You see it, and it's like you've seen it before, but you just don't know what to do with it. It's been what? Seven years, eight years now? It's been a long time. I was like, man, I've got to go

back to school, just take a class, any class, just to get your mind
thinking again. A lot of people say, 'You got your degree, you
don't need anything else, you just have that paper.' But really, it's
something more than that. Just anything! Just get your mind
thinking again. I think I would choose anything. Now, in order
for them to pay for it, I would have to choose something that's in
my field, but I don't care what it is, really. As long as I'm thinking, I'm doing something. There's this old guy, he just had a
heart murmur. And sometimes we will sit down and talk—I
mean he's like a dictionary! This guy knows it all. He's been
everywhere, he was in the armed forces. He knows everything!
He would tell about a topic, he would just talk about it. You
know, you say, 'What about the deserts'? He say, 'Well, you got
three major deserts; you got the Sahara, the Gobi, and you got
the Arabian.' And he talk forever, forever, forever, and he said
the best way to learn, and he say, 'This is what I do,' the best way
to learn is to read. That's what he says. 'I read all the time.' And
he said 'What about Benjamin Franklin? How did people like
him learn? They didn't have teachers, they read! They got a little
candle and lit it up and started reading.'

"I told my wife that I was reading an article and it said that
they were doing a little survey, that they started reading when a
baby was about six months old; they started reading a book a
day. The baby is not going to comprehend or anything, but just
reading, reading, and they did that until the baby was about two
years old; and they took another survey where they didn't read to
the baby; and they said that the other baby that was read to
caught on so fast. . . . So I told my wife, I'm going to start reading to Alexis, you know." He laughed. "When she gets six
months, she's going to get read to every day. When they get
about one, when they can understand, you can ask questions,
you know: 'What have you learned today?' They can't say anything—it's just getting them to participate, and getting them to
learn that way, and they say that increase their learning ability.
That's what I missed. I didn't get—my parents had encyclope-

dias, you know, accessible to us, and we looked at them all the time, but I never got read to. And every time I go home, where my nieces and that, I read to them, so I think that's what I'm going to do. I mean you've got to stay abreast of that, you've got to stay on that.

"I think one thing, I think you should put less emphasis on math in high school, in elementary school, I mean because I'm telling you—I mean reading, writing—that should be the main curriculum. You read, you write, because that's what you're going to use when you get out. You got to use reading; you always will have to know how to write, always have to know how to read. Those things are going to be with you forever. But as far as math—I don't know what's—unless that's what you're going to school for, engineering or math teacher or that—but as far as anything else—I've never seen an algebra problem since I've been out of school. I think if you know how to read, I think if you know how to write, then that communication—I mean that's all about communicating. If you know how to do that, communication will come so easy; it's going to be natural."

At this point, I could not resist reminding Lenny of the complaint he had made twelve years earlier and asking him if he felt a more multicultural curriculum would have made a difference to him.

"Did I say that!!?? 'Black people can't learn English'??!! Gaaawww dog! Naw, I don't think another curriculum would have made a difference. Because if you didn't learn that one then, I don't think—I mean, what kind of other curriculum? I mean, based on what? If you don't learn English or writing—that's always going to be in the curriculum. African studies program? All right, that's good! But you're still going to have to have English to read it. That's why I'm shocked that I said that." He laughed again. I could already hear him telling Marinette or the guys at work about this. "I probably really didn't see English, proper English, in high school. If you don't see anything in high school, then how are you going to learn anything in college? You have to start at an early age, I mean you just can't come to college and say 'I'm going to learn a lot.' It has to be with you; you can't skip high school and go to college. I probably didn't see it. But you know, white people have different types of English too. I know a lot of people that say 'Gaaww, he sounds like he's white.' I mean what's that? I mean, if you speak the correct way, then there's only one way to speak. You know, I just don't see it when somebody says, 'He can't even talk. Well, that's the way they talk anyway, so let him talk,' you know? A lot of people do that as a matter of fact—'Well don't you know how they talk?' Naw, there's no white language, there's no black language, you speak the English language and that's it. There's different dialects; you hear southern people talking in that southern drawl; you go to Boston, you hear a different dialect, but it's the same English-speaking system.

"Another thing I want for Alexis, what I want her to do is learn another language. I told this guy, my partner at work, I was saying, 'I want to get my daughter to learn another language.' He's like—'Why?' He's like—'Just get her to learn English.' I was like, 'No, if she wants to learn Spanish—I don't care what she wants to learn, but learn another language, because that's so important.' I never realized that's so important—I mean so you can travel! You can go somewhere else and you can just fit in there with them. Just be bilingual. That's what I've heard, if you start young, it will be so easy. Twenty, thirty, will be too hard.

"And I want her mind made up before she even—because that's the key, if you make your mind up when you're young, what you want to do, and stick with it. I really want her to know what she wants to be and work for that goal when she's young, not waiting until college, not waiting until—you know, in high school, she should start to think. And if she makes her mind up to be something, yeah, it may change, but still she at least has that idea, and that's something positive; it's something you put in your daughter, or your children—it's something positive to make them work on something. And I want her to be independent.

That's what I want her to get from me. Don't ever let anybody say you can't do that. I don't ever want to tell my daughter that you can't do that; I might tell her it's going to be hard, it's going to take a lot of work, but I don't want to say—'Well, you can't do that—just give up.' Because you never know what they're thinking."

The huge television screen had been flickering in silence, tuned into live coverage of the Miami–Colorado game. Suddenly, out of the corner of my eye, I saw that a brawl had broken out between the teams, and Lenny and I turned to watch as more and more players streamed from the sidelines onto the field to join the fray.

"That's amazing," said Lenny delightedly. "That is giving them such a bad name." He began to laugh. "They've already got such a bad name. They've got a name for fighting; see, this is what they expect of this team. 'Hey! They think we're going to fight, let's fight!'"

"That's another thing," said Lenny, turning back to the conversation when the fracas had ended. "When I got to F.S.U., people walk around like, 'Yeah, I play football, yeah,' you know. If you're not really that way, you're going to do it because that's what they expect. You live up to expectations. They stereotype you. It's a stereotype world. It's like you're not supposed to make good grades—you're a football player. The system, the school, is the same, and if the system doesn't see that—I mean, those statistics you hear, about why so many blacks fail—because the system, they don't expect you—because they look at your color and they say 'I don't expect him to do that well in this, I'm just going to push him through. If he barely makes it, then that's good'—so they just push you along, and the guy who they're pushing along, he says, 'Well, I made it. Hey!' You know. 'I made it.' He don't look at, 'Well, I missed something. What did I miss?' No, he's like—'I made it. Why should I care what I missed? That's history.' But when that test comes about, then it's like, 'Yeah, I missed a lot. Look what all I missed. I'm below a seventh-grade level. But I'm in eleventh grade.' What does that say about the system? They have some people that graduated from high school and can't even read. But how ... how ... *how* can you get through high school without reading? That's what's wrong with the system there. And what about Florida? Florida is below ... Florida is down—Florida is below *Alabama*. I mean this is the biggest place, you have so much money here, and we're down at the bottom, I mean at the bottom of the, I think, the third lowest. And what can you do? What's the answer?

"For one thing, teachers don't get paid here. They feel 'Hey, why should I teach? I'm not getting paid.' And the parents don't really care; the parents have to work all the time, because they have to support these kids, so the kids don't have any guidance. They get home, they throw their books in the corner and go and play. It's always sunny outside; they go to the beach. What's a book? That's the mentality here. It's not—this state is not an education state. It's not, because you got so many obstacles. You got the weather, you got the thinking, you got—I mean you got so many things. You got money—money is a big issue too. I mean it's like who cares? Who cares? That's the feeling here in Florida—who cares? The only reason why people go to school is—'Gosh, I wish I were going to school so I could make more money.' That's the only reason. It's not saying, 'What do you want to be?' 'I want to be this.' No, it's like, 'I want to make money.' Money. They don't go to school to learn. They go to school just to get over it. People only look at money: 'I'm going to be an engineer—that pays sixty thousand dollars.' They don't say, 'I'm going to be a nurse, because I like to do that, I like the work, I like to take care of people.' Even though they're unhappy, because of the money that's what they wanted to do. And people respect you for your occupation. If you don't have a job, they don't want to know what you know. Because they figure if you don't have a job, you don't know anything. You may have got that job through somebody's father—but they only look at the job, your occupation, what you do. In the U.S.A., and here in

Florida, it's really who you know. And kids know that nowadays. Their parents say, 'You just go to school, you do this, and I'll let you just have my company.' You know, black kids can't do that, because they don't have the parents to give them that; they have to go out and get a job. They got to compete. You got to compete with your records, and if your records aren't good, you're going to be dropped.

"A black kid has so many obstacles, I mean he has so many; I'm not saying only because he's black, but he has so many obstacles. That's why I said, if a black man makes it, then I mean that guy needs to be—he's worked his butt off in order to make it. I mean you respect a black man who's made it because what he's been through, you don't know. Because of his race. I'm not saying it's not achievable, but it's much harder for a black man to do it than for a white man, because this is a white man's world. He's only going to let you go where he wants you to go.

"I think a lot of white people, they look at black people and they judge it by this color. Because a lot of white people don't have black friends. They don't. They don't know what a black person is—the only black people they see is on this TV right here, and they see the news. A black man killed a white motorcyclist. You know, a black man doing this, a black man doing that—all negative. They see this all on television. They see this and it's ingrown, and then once they see a real black person it's like they're scared!" Lenny started to laugh. " 'Oohhoo . . . what is he going to do? He might take my car. Let me lock my doors, lock it, see if it's locked!' See, that's the problem. See that's—it goes back a long ways, it goes back so far, it's just ingrown. Because I got this friend, he always tells me that 'I'm not racist.' I'm like, 'Don't give me that bull.' He's like, 'Man, I got black friends, I got black—I used to hang out with black people.' I'm like, 'You *are* racist. I mean, you can't sit here and tell me that you're not racist, because everybody's racist.' Everybody. Everybody has a little fire of it. It's just somebody's fire burns more than others—that's all it is. It's just a little fire. But you are racist.

That fire is there in everybody. And once something happens, when you go to New York and you are scared, that fire is strong. Because in a peaceful society, you're just comfortable, and it's a little fire. You go to New York and see a black man, you're— 'Oh! What's he going to do?' " Lenny laughed. "And that's the way it is. And the answer? I don't know the answer, I mean because it goes back a hundred years. It goes back so far. And they didn't find a solution, why should we? And this friend, you know I kid with him—'Hi, racist.' He gets so mad! But I tell him, 'Hey, boy—everybody is racist. I'm a little racist.' He thought a little and said, 'Well, I am a little prejudiced.' " Lenny laughed delightedly. " 'I'm not racist, I'm a little prejudiced!' He kiss all the black babies that come by, he kiss 'em—'Yeah, look it—I'm not racist!'

"You know, I go in a courtroom, and I look at those prisoners and out of thirty prisoners, you got twenty-five of them black; you got two that are Hispanic and you got one white. I'm not saying that's wrong. Who knows, who knows what it is? I think it's partly the system, partly the economics. And you got the judicial system. I mean it's such a mess—they let people out, it's just a wreck in the courthouse. I mean you see people walking out like—'Yeah, I got over it.' You know, they laugh at the system! Yeah, it's a total joke. They *laugh* at the system. I'll tell you what, they have a jail here that has all carpeting, wall-to-wall carpeting, a bigger TV than this, big huge TV, they got a weight room that's humongous, I mean there's no deterrent. When you get in this prison, you're not going to want to go out. They want to go back to prison. They get three meals a day, they have it all. You got carpet, you got everything you want, you got your freedom— yeah, it's freedom. It's freedom in jail; out here is where you're not free; that's the way they feel. Because out here you got to find a place to live, you got to take care of your children, you got to find money. That's not free. I bet that if you changed the whole system, where you put them in chain gangs, get them digging ditches all day long, in this one-hundred-degree weather, I'll bet you—I mean there would be some blacks in there, but it wouldn't be like it is now. It's like a joke to them. They're talking, they stand up in front of the judge like, 'What are you going say now? Back to prison? All right! See ya.' It has to change, it has to change.

"Just like the thirteen-year-old boy, you know, the one that killed that tourist here in Florida; he had a record as long as this room here. Thirteen years old. He has a record out of this world. Who's going to give him a job?"

"Does he deserve a job?" I asked. "Do you blame someone for not hiring him?"

"That's true," said Lenny. "But you have to give that guy an opportunity. What is he going to do? What else can he do? So do you blame him? What else can you do for him to get out of this situation? He got his chance at twelve? What are you saying?" he demanded, suddenly agitated. "He got his chance at twelve? The first offense he make—you got to be stringent. You can't slap him on the hand and say, 'All right'—slap—'go ahead.' The first offense—you do something about it. The second offense—hey, bam! You send him back to a boot camp. I mean as tough—you make him break rocks, you make him just bust his butt, anything. And then if he does it again, you send him to a harder place—make it harder. Don't make it easier, make it harder. If you just slap him on his hand, what's going to stop him? What's going to stop him? The system just rides them along, just push them along, and just let them do what they want to do. And that's the problem. See, the first offense, this kid, he shouldn't never have had fifty-six offenses. That's the system. That goes to show you that it's the system—it's him also, but if this guy has committed fifty-six—I mean, what does the judge do? What does he do? What does he say when he sees all these crimes committed? I mean, he sees all this list, and the forty-fifth one he's like, 'Well, all right, go ahead'? He has the same sheet that we see. It's no secret. It's not like saying, 'Gaawwwleee—he has fifty-six of them? I didn't know this; I thought he had one.' If we know, I know he knows. So it's his fault. Let's just face it, this guy has fifty-six arrests, and he kept doing the same thing over and over again, and this judge keep sending him out, sending him out the door, that's his fault too. He ought to be convicted. They ought to put the judge on trial. Put the judge there and say, 'Hey, you let this guy off fifty-six times, we gonna put you in the boot camp.'" Lenny laughed, but shook his head. "Thirteen years old. Fifty-six crimes, and it ends in murder. Who's to blame? Is it that kid there? Yes. Is it the system? Yes. Is it the judge? Yes. It's all the above. Is it the parents? Yes. It's so many things that you can say yes on. I mean, everybody has their hand in. My partner and I, we talk about this all the time. We said we're going to write Clinton and try to get the system changed.

"That's what the young people have to face now, and I feel sorry. I feel sorry for *her*. It's just *different*. That's why I was so reluctant of having kids, you know, because raising them in a society like this, I mean like, they've got *so much* to deal with. It's unreal. You got peer pressure, you have got so much— you've got all that's on TV, you've got all of this. Ten years ago, you didn't have all this. What about ten years from now, the year 2000? What's it going to be like? What can you do? I don't see anything—what can you, what can you do about it? I don't . . . I don't . . . I don't see—is it so gone you just can't do anything? I mean, could you bring it back? I mean, is it reachable? I don't think you can do that anymore. I think you can just ride the bad wave and see what happens, and if everybody's on their feet, then try it over again."

The bedroom door opened and Marinette and her mother came out, Marinette still holding Alexis.

"My wife has to go back to work in a couple of weeks," said Lenny, watching the women say their good-byes at the door. "She cries and cries every time she thinks of leaving the baby. And me—see, I'm working so much, you know. My regular job is from seven-thirty until four o'clock, and then I go to another job from five-thirty until nine p.m. So I'm constantly working now; I've been doing this for about four months now. It's paying the bills, you know, but still, I don't have the opportunity to see my daughter. And I don't really have the opportunity to do anything like weight-lift, stuff like that. I really miss that. When I come home, I can't work out, because I got to see my daughter, to see my family, and I'm missing them as it is. So when I get home, I sort of stay here and play with them a little, be a father. But I got to make some money though."

"Have you seen the pictures of Lenny when he was working out?" said Marinette, turning from the door and catching the last part of the conversation. She disappeared into the bedroom to deposit Alexis and returned with a wedding album which showed photographs of Marinette dressed in a bridal gown with an unrecognizable man by her side: Lenny Chavers, slim and athletic, but with a lean, ordinary face that was creased deeply on either side of his mouth as if it had just collapsed.

"I don't like him so much like that," said Marinette, reading my thoughts. "He's not so jolly." Throughout this inspection, Lenny stood looking on somewhat awkwardly but on the whole pleased. About his bodybuilding experience he was unabashed.

"I went from a forty-two-inch waist to a twenty-nine-inch waist," he said, finding his voice and quickly becoming expansive on the subject. "My chest was forty-eight inches. My body ripped, it just took off. In the Mr. Tallahassee competition, people were telling me I was looking good. I had the chest, but I didn't have the legs ("ow, ouch . . ."). It would be hard to get to that next stage without using steroids, and I don't want to do that. But you can't compete with the guys who do drugs— it's like it makes them complete. I have a tape of the Mr. Tallahassee competition," he recalled, his face brightening, and he set about sifting through the videotapes stored under the television set.

Some minutes later, he was sitting on the floor in perplexity, with all the tapes spread around him.

"Lenny, I think you lent it to your friend," said Marinette gently.

"I know I'll find it as soon as you go," said Lenny glumly. It was the only situation I had ever seen from which he was unable to extract some degree of humor.

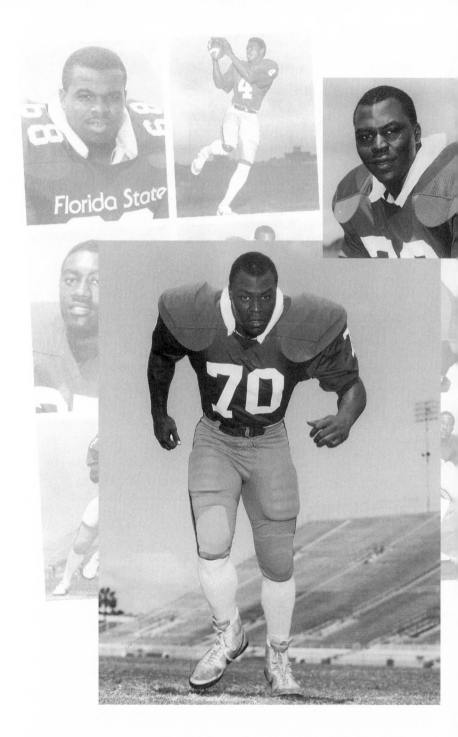

Florida State

PAT

"I first saw Pat Woolfork in the summer, when he was workin' on the roads. I thought he was a *criminal*, a chain-gang *criminal*," said John Feagin one night, punching his hand with a fist, while the other players laughed in recognition of the characterization. Pat was big, burly, and round-shouldered. In winter, dressed in a dark padded jacket and his knit cap, he looked like the Dickensian burglar who thumps people over the head in dark alleys.

Despite his appearance, Pat was taciturn and retiring—a "close study"—and not at all aggressive. He tended to keep to himself, usually coming to study hall on his own; if the class was joking among themselves, he might give signs of listening to the others, perhaps even showing some amusement, but he would rarely interject any comment of his own.

One evening, as Lenny Chavers was leaving the study room in his usual high spirits, he made a crack about Pat's knit cap. "He just sit there with his old Buddha head—yeah, *Buddha head,*" said Lenny, rocking with laughter and all set to flog this subject ad infinitum. An ugly and uncharacteristic silence suddenly froze the room. People looked out of the corner of their eyes at one another, and Lenny's jolly laugh died away on his face.

"You want to tell another joke?" said Pat, looking up from his workbook.

"No," said Lenny, hand on the doorknob, and somewhat bewildered.

" 'Cos we all laughing," said Pat.

Nothing of Pat's personality came through in his workbook exercises, and he made so few comments in class that I never really got a handle on him. I did come to see that he preferred dealing with people one-on-one, however, and didn't have the interest or the instinct for the usual group dynamics, which gave him the—perhaps false—air of being a loner.

After the class had finished the grammar workbooks and moved on to writing essays, Pat formed a close attachment to another tutor, and I had little more interaction with him.

Nonetheless, I had a few surprising glimpses into what lay behind that formidable and intimidating exterior. Once, in talking about possible degree majors, Pat volunteered the astonishing fact that he would like to major in art. He was very specific: he wanted to be an illustrator, and for many years had drawn cartoons and comics to entertain his nieces and nephews. Sadly, the exigencies of his schedule were such that I did not see him realistically getting to even one of these courses for another year and a half. But I had caught in Pat's usually impassive face a glimmer of privately harbored dreams and ambitions—indeed, of unexpected youth— and although I never saw one of his drawings, I was ready to believe he had real talent: I don't think he would have allowed himself to be vulnerable to this dream if he had not. Above all, however, I remember walking away from this conversation and thinking to myself, "So, Pat's got a soft spot for children."

Pat's parents were still at their old address and phone number, and I had no trouble contacting them. But I was in for a surprise. All the other players had stayed in close touch with at least their mothers, but Pat's family had no idea where he was.

"He went to Bristol—Bristol, Pennsylvania," his mother said, when I first reached her. "I sure would like to hear from him, but I figure if he was in trouble, I'd hear."

For the next two years, I checked in with Mrs. Woolfork after every holiday—Thanksgiving, Christmas, birthdays—thinking that, prompted by either duty or sentiment, Pat might have called her on these occasions, but I met with no success. A brother was also trying to find him, as were some cousins.

"His brother is thinking of contacting the Red Cross," his mother said.

Pat left F.S.U. after his second year and joined the army. He was stationed for three years in Korea before coming home and then moving on to Bristol, where he had a girlfriend.

"She wrote to me," said Mrs. Woolfork. "She was expecting a child. I may be a grandmother."

I tried tracking the girlfriend through her last known address, but as I learned from telephone information, it was two years out of date; she was at a new address now, with an unlisted number.

"Do you remember where she worked?" I asked Mrs. Woolfork, certain that this girlfriend was the critical link and hoping to trace her through her job.

"Oh, I don't believe she works," Mrs. Woolfork replied, bringing me to another dead end.

Pat had once worked as a roofer, so I called every roofing company in Bristol. All the managers I spoke with seemed to be Irish, and although I received no information whatsoever about Pat, a great deal of commentary was volunteered regarding the superiority of Notre Dame to Florida State.

"Do you think Patrick would still be working out?" I asked Mrs. Woolfork; I had it in mind to check out all the gyms in Bristol.

"Oh no, honey, he got over that a long time ago," she said.

He had worked in a supermarket—at least, a friend of a cousin had heard that someone had seen him in one.

"Do you know in what part of town he was seen?" I asked the cousin. No, he didn't know; in fact, the friend wasn't really sure it was Patrick.

Army records; social security; public assistance; jails—nothing yielded any information.

And at the end of every conversation, Pat's mother would say wistfully, "I don't know why he don't just call."

ORSON

When I finally got hold of Orson by telephone, he said during the course of our conversation something about having different views on life now that he was thirty and not eighteen. I was taken aback—not by the thought that he, or anyone else I had tutored, could be thirty years old, but by the reminder that he had been eighteen when I had first met him, a fact I still found impossible to absorb. I had always thought of Orson as being "grown"—certainly, twelve years ago, closer to thirty than eighteen. This perception was in great part provoked by his sheer physical dimensions—six feet five inches in height and two hundred and fifty pounds—which it didn't seem conceivable to attain in only eighteen years.

But the illusion of age was manifest in more meaningful respects as well. Like Billy Allen, Orson had grown up in a city—in his case, Miami—and what life had taught him in eighteen years on its hard, fast-moving, reckless streets was not to be compared with what one could learn by eighteen in, say, Milton, Florida. Or by twenty-five in Tallahassee; clearly, I now realize, the main reason Orson seemed older than he was was my sense that he seemed older than me.

In dress and manner, Orson already called to mind the man he

surely would become: a genial, bearish family man in knee-length
shorts and a sports shirt, a plastic mug of beer or Coca-Cola in
his hand, barbecuing on weekends. He turned up for tutorial sessions holding his plastic F.S.U. logo-inscribed mug of Coke with
the air of a man who has come to play cards or talk sports with
the boys. His small twinkling eyes betrayed a playful nature, but
I also saw that, even at eighteen, rubbed up against the wrong
personality he would be intimidating. From odds and ends I
picked up from the other players, I gathered that Orson was considered by the Football Office to be "difficult." I understood that
this did not necessarily mean that he had caused actual difficulties, but that the coaches were keenly aware that a potential
showdown with Orson would not be guaranteed, for all their authority, to end to their advantage. Several members of the football staff were short white men who had never realized the
dreams of athletic glory that can characterize their kind, and for
them, I imagined, an Orson Mobley—big, brawny, black, talented, and apparently uncomprehending of his position in the
hierarchy of power that was supposed to regulate the relationship between them—represented the embodiment of some exis-
tential nightmare.

Which is not to say that I didn't now and then pick up hints of
real trouble spots. On one occasion, Orson came to study hall
snapping at people, in a brusque bad mood, and no stretch of the
imagination accommodated the delusion that he would that
night sit quietly at a table and do his homework for two hours
like a good boy. My feeling was that as long as he didn't disturb
me or anyone I was working with, there was nothing to be gained
by troubling with him, but at some point in the evening he approached me and apologized for his behavior, holding up his
plastic mug and telling me he was drunk—and adding that I
should blame "them" for driving him to drink, for making him
act this way. By "them" he meant the coaches. But why, I wondered, were the pressures on Orson Mobley more intense than
those on other players? Was he serious or just playing? Was he

even really drunk? Some of the others told me Orson drank, so it was altogether possible, although his behavior and speech struck me at that moment as being overly calculated. But whether drunk or not, the incident suggested problems I hadn't until then suspected.

In terms of schoolwork pure and simple, I never felt that, relative to the other players, Orson was so badly prepared. He could write coherent paragraphs, although after those coherent opening paragraphs he simply petered out, gave up. I remember a particular ghost story about vampire bats, which he called "Bambire"—"You know, that's how those old black men say it when they're telling stories"—and the conversation took off on an interesting tangent, a tangent that would have made a valid addition to the story had it ever been written, but which, as it never was, remained totally beside the point. But that was Orson, wresting an assignment off track with more effort and energy than he would have needed to complete it properly. When his interest in some proposition was lacking, there was simply nothing to be done, as he was beyond being bullied, cajoled, or threatened. Without hostility or rancor, indeed with a certain charm, he would simply turn his attention somewhere else, tell engaging stories, laugh kindly, almost paternally, at me, and go his way.

Even so, I ran into Orson sitting under a tree outside the football apartment shortly after I had officially stopped tutoring, and seeing me approach he got to his feet to meet me, carefully dusting the earth off his hands as he did so. "I just want to thank you for all you tried to do for me. I surely do appreciate it," he said, and held his hand out for me to shake.

Orson was one of the two players, the other being Jessie Hester, whom I heard about over the years from sources other than the most devoted Florida State football fans. Orson had been drafted to the Denver Broncos, and I saw his name from time to time in the sports pages; then I heard he was with the Colts; then the reports became confused—he was with Miami, he was back with the Colts; there had been problems with alcohol and drugs. . . .

"As a matter of fact," his agent said, when I reached him by telephone, "I don't know where he is. He left Miami and hasn't stayed in touch." Through information, I located his mother in Jacksonville, where she had moved from Miami with her own mother after Hurricane Andrew destroyed her home. Orson was, as it turned out, now living with the two of them.

"Orson played with the Broncos for a while," his grandmother told me, the first time I called their home. It was his day off and he had left early that morning to go fishing. "Then he went to Indiana, but then, he just let it drop. Orson never did like pain," she said, laughing gently. "He's got a job now—I think it's selling cars. It would be good for you to talk with him. He needs confidence. He's just discouraged—he's got so much, but he's just discouraged these days.

"In the pros, he was called the Big O. If he doesn't tell you that, be sure to put it in your book."

Orson's mother's home was in a typical Florida suburb of low, flat-roofed bungalows set in modest gardens, a quiet family neighborhood. The friend who had driven me on this trip instinctively drew up at a house outside which was parked a big brown-gold van emblazoned with cowboy drawings. "A pro player's wheels," he said decisively, and switched off the engine. He was right, and I was greeted at the front door by Orson's mother, a woman almost as tall as Orson, very lively and very friendly. She described the noise of the hurricane bearing down upon her home—the wind roaring, *whoooo*, "like a wild animal was at the door, like a monster," while she and her family ran from room to room, literally trying to hold the roof on. "Ours was the only home on the block to survive; I think it was because my faith was stronger."

It was late December, and a Christmas tree bedecked with angels and snowmen dominated the living room, presiding over a pile of presents, among which pride of place was given to a Shirley Temple doll. This, as Orson's mother told me, was an original and had been recently restored, freshly clothed, angelic, white. While I was admiring it, Orson himself came in, filling the doorway, his head slightly bowed as if used to ducking ceilings. He looked to me not older but tireder, his eyes and face kind, but with the impish sparkle, the impudence, gone from them.

His greeting was matter-of-fact, and we moved into the dining area, passing the doorway to the den, which was hung with his football photographs.

"What exactly do you want?" he asked when we were seated, not unfriendly, but in the manner of a man who has moved in hard circles and has learned to ask for the bottom line at the outset. He sat as of old, slightly hunched forward from long habit of trying to meet others on their own level, his big hands loose between his knees. "OK," he said resignedly, focusing on the task at hand, The Interview. His face, I realized, now looked its actual age. When he spoke, the tumbling words fell out in a quick patter (that would best be transcribed on paper without any punctuation at all), his voice rarely changing inflection, narrating all events, opinions, feelings, in the same factual tone, warming to his task as time went on but never growing confidential.

"Well, with me, I got a scholarship to Florida State, not really being prepared for college at all. I played like one year high school football, you know, that was my senior year, I always played baseball before that; yeah, I played baseball for two years—I was drafted by the Expos out of high school, but I was drafted late, because I signed a letter of intent to go to Florida State. I was definitely not prepared for college, as far as high school, you know, as far as studying, because I got by in class being semi-intelligent, not studying, not really knowing how to study, and then getting up there to Florida State.

"It was kind of funny because the school I went to in high school was really a predominantly white school and they sent athletes out; they sent all the black athletes to black colleges, and then they tried to get the white athletes into Florida State and places like that. But then our defensive coach came along and he had a relationship with one of the coaches at Florida State because he had a couple of players go there and he was basically the only reason why I ended up playing there. I was just fortunate because the one white guy that they were looking at, he broke his leg, tore up his knee, so Florida State asked was there anybody else we had on the team that they could take a look at.

"High school was fun, I have a lot of good memories, and some bad ones. It used to be an all-boys school and the head coach he was, I mean, he was a redneck, it was just plain and simple, that's what he was. There was racism in other aspects, but as long as you were playing sports and you could do something for them, you know, they pretty much let you do what you want to do.

"At my high school, we have a wall of fame—a Wall of Fame—and they have a few requirements you have to get to make it on there, it's pretty prestigious for a high school: you got to go to State in two different sports, and different requirements. Well, they came down to me; I had won the athlete of the year for Dade County and Miami, so that brings prestige to the school, and our football team had won the sports award and the school that wins that gets this big award, this big trophylike plaque. And we won that that year, but I wasn't good enough to get on the Wall of Fame, 'cos it came down to first they said it was this reason, then it was that, then it came all the way down to who had the best grade point average, so a white girl that was a tennis player won out over me; and to this day I'm not up there, and there was a big deal about it because the lady that's the athletic director now, she used to be a P.E. teacher, she tried to get me to come back out there and she said, 'I could do something about it now, back then I couldn't do anything about it.' And I kind of told her, you know, it's no big deal, I didn't really put too much emphasis on that anyway.

"I enjoyed high school, I wish I could go back; I had some good times there, it wasn't all that bad, I just wish I could have asserted myself more in the classroom, like I do when I play football, or baseball, or basketball, or anything I was competitive in, but I didn't take that same competitiveness into the classroom. Hard to say why not. I wish I could say. My mom always, when I was young, made me do my homework, you know, she stayed on me to get good grades or I couldn't play sports, but I got the good grades so I could play the sports instead of really getting the good grades to have the good grades; it was like I know I got to do good in this class if I want to play sports.

"I pretty much taught myself to play sports, you know, it was just me and my mom; my parents were separated and I was born after my father went off into the service. I really don't know him. And it was times when she got out there and tried to throw me baseballs when I was little—she did it all, she tried to. My brother, he helped some, but he could not pitch, he was wild, he threw balls everywhere behind me, and I'd be out there an hour before I got to hit about ten balls." Orson laughed, rubbing his hands on his shorts, loosening up.

"Kids I grew up with in the neighborhood, we used to play different games, and I watched TV and I watched the pros play and I'd just go out there and do what they did—I guess I was blessed to be gifted to pick up games pretty quick. My tenth-grade year, I just played baseball, I didn't play anything else. That's my first love. And my second year, I played baseball and basketball. I only played football in my senior year.

"I don't think there was anything much that would have got my attention in high school—I think it would have had to come from me. Right now, my education doesn't affect my life, it doesn't, but the way everything is now, it's very important to have a degree. I want to go back and finish up my degree—I think I have like a year left. I was a criminal justice major. Criminal justice kind of interests me. That's one thing I really got into; I like to read those true detective magazines and stuff like that, suspense novels, I just kind of get into stuff like that. Like right now, I'm reading this book called *Search for the Green River Killer*, and stuff like that is just intriguing to me, you know, just to hear the different ways the police investigate different cases and how they research—different things they do as far as getting in this person's head without actually knowing who he is, how he thinks, and why is he committing these murders, and that type of stuff. I don't know if it's real or not, but I like stuff like that. I just got the book a couple of days ago and I get to reading it and it's just like it's hard to put down. I wouldn't want to be a police officer though, but maybe one day I could get into federal security somehow. I did well in my criminal justice courses, I was interested in them and I was always there and I paid attention; other classes, I really didn't. I knew I had to be there, so that's why I basically went, but the difference between night and day, you know, a criminal justice course and an elective course, it was just different, it was night and day compared to my interest level."

My question as to whether there was anything he remembered from the English classes or from our tutorials was met with an explosion of loud laughter.

"Not much. Not much. Like I said, back then I really didn't put a big emphasis—I looked at it actually as a job, you know, I had to be there and there weren't no ifs, ands, or buts about it, and I put in my time and after it was over I didn't think about it. That's sad to say, but that's just how I felt. I know I could have been a good student, you know, I'm pretty intelligent and I pick things up pretty quick, and for me to get through as far in school as I did, with the least amount of effort I put into it"—he laughed heartily again—"well, that's an accomplishment in itself if you want to look at it that way. But I think if I'd have put forth the effort and really tried, I think I could have been a B student, maybe even an A student.

"Is there anything I regret I didn't learn in school? I would say writing. Just being able to do it when you need to, and then putting together different letters and stuff like that, résumés, and different type stuff. Math! I never did care for math and—I mean as long as you can count well enough to manage your money, you know, that's really all you need. But writing is very important. I wish—I know in college, I used to write terrible letters and I still do. My nephew, he reads a lot and I think that's great; I wish I would have started reading when I was a lot younger because there is so much you can learn just by reading, whether it's just maybe a book like yours, or an autobiography by an athlete, you know, there's a lot of stuff out there. Like I like to read myself these suspenseful novels, or the good juicy books—that type of stuff, something that really catches my interest. If it's something not very interesting that I start reading, then I put it down, I lose interest—that type of deal. I found in reading, I learned words, you know, learned meanings of words, just by reading it.

"As far as Florida State, I guess, I don't know, I guess it kind of snuck up on me, my unpreparedness, 'cos many times I was able to get away with a lot of stuff and still being able to pass the class; but if I'd have put forth the effort in those classes I could have had some good grades. But I guess it kind of snuck up on me, when I get behind and when I really needed to have a good semester, you know, to carry the 3.0 for that semester—that was the only way I could stay in school—I found myself being over my head then, and I felt like 'I'm over my head now.' I remember studying and preparing for a test and I mean, just fully preparing for a test and getting in there and getting a C on the first test, I mean totally prepared for it, and I studied, you know, I done everything I was supposed to do and then going back and taking it two more times and getting D's! It's kinda discouraging. I knew right then I was in trouble, and I never understood why my adviser would put me in a class like that. You know, seems like at the time when I was on academic probation and that I needed to take some classes to get my grades up, I found myself in a class for biology that forty percent of the class don't do well—it's the big auditorium class.

"You're right; I relied on people telling me what to take. That's my fault. But it's like being a regular student there, it probably would have been different, especially if you had to pay your own way—which I wouldn't have been able to do—but I'm just saying with grants and different things you can look and you can take a class that's going to interest you; but when you're playing football, you know, you got a certain time frame and there's only a limited amount of classes that you can take in that time frame; you can't take a night class 'cos you got either study hall or you got films, you know, it's got to be in between that eight to one or two o'clock area, before you're practicing.

"I knew growing up, if I didn't get the grades, if I didn't go to school, I couldn't play sports. So I did the same when I got to college, you know, I just did well enough just to skate by for a couple of years, but then when my back was up against the wall I didn't know how to then, I mean, I was at literally over my head. Finally, there was those two subjects and I had a D in one, and an F in the other, and that dropped me down, where I was already on academic probation, and it was either summer school or junior college; and to go to summer school, I was told you had to talk to the dean, and if the dean gave you permission to go to summer school to get the credits you needed you could; but if he didn't feel that you were ready to meet the academic requirements, then he would tell you that you need to go down to junior college. I can remember this one little guy that played free safety for us, I think he was like flunking two or three classes like me, and he was allowed to stay there and go to summer school. I went and talked to the dean, and you know, I knew him pretty well and he told me, he just said 'I don't have anything to do with this—it's not me.' So I had an opportunity to go to summer school given the permission to, but instead I was told that I needed to go down and get my A.A. and then I would be welcome back.

"Bobby Bowden wanted me to be a football player, a football

player and a football player only. And this is the conversation we had when we—see, first of all, Bobby Bowden came down to my house; he sat in my kitchen and ate food there and I told him I'm thinking about the University of Miami—which I really wasn't, because I lived in Miami all my life and I wanted to get away from Miami, but I didn't want to go too far, so it was either Florida State or the University of Miami. Florida State was a likely choice, you know, I watched it growing up, and I was just intrigued with the school. And Bobby said, 'Oh yeah, you can play baseball, yeah, no problem with that, we don't have any problem; you play football, and baseball the rest of the year,' and then when I got there it was out and out—I was told that, you know, Coach Young was going to give me a dual scholarship, double scholarship. I had did things like run Frazer's baseball camp— he was the coach of the University of Miami, he's retired now, but as a youth I did his camps, where I taught, you know, I helped out with the kids and stuff, and so I wouldn't have had any problem playing baseball, or football either, with the University of Miami. But at Florida State, I had to first make the baseball team and then after my first year, I had to quit and come back for spring and then the second year I was injured and when I got over the injury the football coaches made me quit baseball again; and when I was well, I asked to go back and play 'cos I was playing fairly well up until I was injured that spring. I recovered and Bobby Bowden and me had a meeting in his office and he said—'Well, we need you out here on the football field, so you have to make up your mind,' you know, he said—'I'm the one that feeds you, I'm housing you and I take care of you on a football scholarship—you don't have a baseball scholarship.' So he said, 'If you want to play baseball, you going to do it on your own.' So I said, 'Ooh—wait till my mom hear about how you came to our house and lied,' and he told me, he said—'Ooh— now, you don't have to do all that,' he said, 'it's time for you to grow up, you know, you should be tired of being this mama's boy. Every time something happens you got to call Mama.' Naw, he—in front of the camera, in front of the camera, it's 'gosh' and 'dadgum it' and you know, away from the camera it's 'I'll kick your ass' and this and that." Orson laughed, looking at me in his old avuncular way. "Yes, he does swear. Yes he does, when he's mad, he keeps up that—that's why I say about college football, college football is so competitive now it's *more* than winning; yeah, they punish the kids that don't go to school, but they really don't educate them, you know; they discipline them when they don't go to class, but they don't educate them. They don't take the steps—when I was there, they went through the motions and if you got through the classes—fine; if you didn't, they'd probably find someone that would replace you.

"When I flunked out of—when I was *kicked* out of Florida State—I don't say I flunked out, I say I was kicked out; after I was kicked out of school, I went to school for a while at Dade South Community College; I worked out some in baseball, I was planning about trying to get back into that, but then something just kept telling me, you know, you got something to prove now. Then Terry Bowden got a hold to me and he had a couple of guys already gone up there from Florida State with him, at Salem College, West Virginia—Tracy Ashley and Allen Dale Campbell— and he told me if I went to summer school I would be able to play that year and I wouldn't have to sit out a year, instead of going to a junior college and getting my A.A. and going back to Florida State. So, I decided to do that. I had an opportunity to try for a few baseball teams, but I was determined to get back in school, finish up, and play professional football, that's just what I felt. So when the opportunity came along for me to go up there to Salem, West Virginia, I didn't hesitate; I know it was going to be cold, I knew it was going to be a looong way from home, but I knew I would have a few friends up there. I stopped like this"—he snapped his fingers—"and forgot about baseball.

"You know, after Florida State, then go to this small school, not having all the tutors and the study hall—you know, the training techniques wasn't even the same. It was a private school, and it probably cost just as much to go there as to Florida State. It was one stoplight in the town, very small. It just wasn't the same like Florida State, and I had to just train myself, I had to prepare myself; on holidays, when I went home, I worked out, you know, because I knew I would get a shot at the N.F.L., and I wanted to be prepared; I knew I would have a few scouts looking at me because Terry Bowden had told me that they had a couple at Dallas the year before.

"I left school early because I felt my only opportunity to work out and be in the shape I need to be in was to be at home, because at that time of year in West Virginia it was snowing and I couldn't work outside, I had to work out at a gym and I was limited; and nobody was going to bust doors down to see me doing mathematical equations, or something, but they want to see me what I can do as far as football playing and this is my chance and if this don't work out I can always go back to school—you know that saying—'Well, I can always go back.' I felt like I made that decision and it worked out for me; I went home and I didn't do it just to quit school; I went home and I worked out twice a day, and I worked out every day, and it paid off for me and I got a chance to play in the N.F.L. for a few years. 'Eighty-six I came home early and I was drafted later on that year, '85, '86, right in there. I was their third pick, but of the sixth round. I was the third overall pick, but the first two rounds they gave up for a trade from the Giants so they picked two guys ahead of me, which was the fourth and fifth round, and I was picked in the sixth. I was a tight end.

"I was there from '86 to '91, and then I went to the Colts. Yeah, I saw Jessie there. Jessie, he had a rocky road, too, as far as the N.F.L. is concerned. He played for a few years, didn't do very well, was released, I think he sat out a year or something, got a second chance with the Colts, and he's been doing real well with them; he's probably one of their mainstays right now. I tried to keep up with most of the guys. Greg Allen, he was just briefly in it, and it was just sad the way his career just dropped. He tore up his knee, and that's after I had left the school and I was playing for Terry Bowden; Greg turned up his knee in a game, and they tried to operate on it, tried to get him back in three weeks for the Florida game and this whole big mess and he wasn't able to play and he had swelling in it, and then he reinjured it, and he ended up with Cleveland; he didn't get drafted high at all—I think he was free agent—and things didn't work out for him. I would have thought for sure he would probably be a first-round pick. I guess everybody—you know, go to college, most everybody, back when I played, you know, you went to college to get to the pros; that was just the way you had to go—you had to go to college in order to get to the pros. That's how I looked at it.

"I was only with the Colts to the end of the year, then I went down to Miami, to see about playing down there. But after the hurricane I moved back up north and stayed with a friend for a while and found out from the Dolphins I hadn't got a place by them, so I had to go out and get a job. I worked for a while at this frozen-food company, worked one of the night jobs; I drove that thing you load the boxes on—a forklift; I operated that for a while, and then my mom told me I always got a room here for you, so I moved here.

"It's . . . it's working OK. You know, when I got here, I just went through the wanted ads, where they said 'Experience is not necessary' and you know I figured—I looked at a few places in Miami but they were only hiring experienced people, and I got up here and this one shop, this one place hires inexperienced people; actually what they do with them, they have them greet the customers, find a vehicle, take them on a demo ride, then when they get them inside they use one of the older guys to close them. And so you split deals, but I've been there like three months now, I get to do some deals myself so it's pretty nice now; you get to dress up, you look important, you feel important—it's a clean job. It's something I can handle. I work probably about fifty, fifty-five hours week, something like that. It's a good job, and not having having many job skills—no job skills, you know,

going to high school, from high school to college, from college to
the pros—you can't acquire any job skills. Like I said, the situation for me is pretty nice, I was very fortunate. It's just something
I like to do, you know, I don't know the car business very well,
but I pretty much know people and that's how I sell my cars. I
sell myself, and I let the car sell itself you know, that's how I do
it. There are some questions that they ask, and I say, 'Ma'am, I
couldn't tell you, but I can find out for you.' I, you know, give
them cards, I still have those football cards with my name on it,
people appreciate those. But I've got to learn the trade and then
I could make some money to live off that if I had to. I guess I feel
pretty lucky right now, being able to do that.

"Like I said, I'd like to finish my degree. Right now, I'm not
into doing it. First, I'm too late, and I'm going to try and get settled exactly what I'm going to be doing, you know, as far as my
life is concerned. I don't expect to be selling cars down the road.
I would like to get back into football in some kind of way if I can,
maybe coach or something like that, or maybe scouting, just
something in football; maybe get on this new team they're going
to have here in Jacksonville. They don't start till '95. By that time
I will be thirty-two going on thirty-three, and not playing for a
few years, but they'll probably have a few older players there,
probably for experience reasons, because they're going to have a
lot of young talent. But the age and not playing you know, that—
can you actually perform on the field? You know, they don't
know that type of stuff; it's a business and they like concrete evidence—'We sign you and know you going to be able to con-
tribute.'

"I have three children of my own. Yeah, they're down in
Miami. I stay somewhat in touch. Two girls and a boy. The
mother, she's doing a fairly good job raising them. The oldest
one, Denise, she told me she wants a computer, that she's using
a computer now in school. Denise is about ten, and she's using a
computer now, so that's what she wants! So I have to try and get
a computer, but it won't be for Christmas though. Right now,

with me traveling and stuff before, and then now I'm here . . .
after the hurricane, I stayed on with my family. I didn't have
transportation, not able to get down there to see them, but, you
know, I talk to them sometimes, just try to make sure everything
is OK. But they're doing fine. Denise, she's real intelligent, and
she enjoys school; I just hope she stays on that mode, because,
you know, for a lot of young kids school is fine when they're
young, but then as they get older it's more work than fun. I hope
she enjoys school the way she do now when she's in high school;
she says she wants to be a lawyer and a doctor—that type of deal.
The only thing I'm probably worrying about is—and you know
there is nothing you can do about it, you can't stop it you know—
is her maybe getting caught up with the wrong guy or something;
down the road it's going to come into play and that's the only
thing I think about. Hopefully, she can hold off until she gets to
college and maybe gets settled in and finishes school, but that's
asking a lot.

"I don't know, maybe if I was a kid nowadays—society itself
is different when it comes to kids—look what you have, you have
strangers that's carrying kids out of their house, you know, that
little girl in California just drug out of the house and just mur-
dered for no reason; I mean if a kid can't feel safe in her own
home, where can you feel safe at? It's . . . it's—I don't know,
the events and stuff, especially this past year with the hurricane
and all the flooding and stuff, it seems like the world is coming
to an end.

"Most of the guys I hung out with, pretty much doing the same
thing they were doing out of high school, maybe working out of
Burdines or something like that, in the warehouse, security,
hanging out, still living with their parents, that type of deal, not
doing anything. Yeah, some of the kids I grew up with, they
know how to sell drugs, and that's all they know how to do, and
that's what they do. And they have families, they feed their families that way, and it's a job for them. That's all they know, and
it's sad when you have to resort to something like that to feed

your family, or to have a roof over your head, but, you know, when you don't have that education, to get the good jobs, nowadays—say I could get a job at McDonald's, but that's for young kids that are starting out, to give them some roots, but you can't support a family working at McDonald's. You know, you work hard, you make maybe two fifty a week; that's good money, but that ain't nothing to build a foundation on. And when you see stuff like that—like me myself, if I got in trouble, who am I going to turn to? I can't turn to my mom, you know; some other kids have that luxury.

"My mom, she brought me up as well as she could; she was very strict, she taught me to know right from wrong, but when I was younger, and still sometime to this day, getting in with, you know, the crowd of people and then they influenced me to do the wrong thing. I drink, you know; they said, 'Well, somebody in your family drink,' which is not true. They said, 'Well, somebody on your father's side.' But *I* did it—that's what I did, wasn't any reason why. And then like my little nephew, he's real smart, but he's the cool type, he likes to walk around and pull his pants down and his mother stays on him and I try to tell him what's happening. Being smart, you know, not being nerdy, he's real sensitive, he worries about kids talking about him, you know, he doesn't fit in, that type of deal. I just hope he doesn't get carried away, you know, like I did, trying to be one of the crowd, having to be liked. I played sports so I didn't need that, but I still had a need to feel that I was liked, you know, and so I done some things that I'm not proud of.

"My mom don't realize that I appreciate everything that she's done for me, 'cos I don't tell her enough. I've been able to do some things for her, like going to Hawaii; I won a couple of trips out there, and going there and jet-skiing and scuba diving, and playing golf—stuff I couldn't have done if I didn't play football, you know, if I didn't go to college, if I didn't play sport, it never would have happened. I went to Jamaica, I had lots of fun there. And we traveled over to Japan and played, we traveled over to

London and played. With the Broncos, yeah. We played at the American Bowl in Japan and we played at the one in London. I have to say I didn't enjoy Japan—it was hot and it was too expensive and there wasn't really anything for you to do if you didn't speak the language; but people are real polite and real clean, and one thing I noticed the whole time I was there, you didn't hear a horn being blowed at another person. We were in a cab and the guy was doing something and the light changed, and the guy just sat there behind him until he looked up—they feel that it's rude to blow at him; but down here, you can look away for a second, the light changes it's like—you find some rude and crude people in vehicles. London was dirty, the people there as a whole, they didn't like Americans and they knew we were football players, because, you know, you don't find too many English people that are tall and big and then just to see a mass of them—it was OK but it wasn't what I dreamed of seeing London on TV. They are definitely not friendly people, no they're not. They're definitely not.

"In the pros, they use you as long as they can, and when they can't use you anymore, they find somebody to replace you. Lot of times, if you're white, you stay within the system, you know, you coach or maybe something like that. I don't experience racism because I'm still looked on as a celebrity, so they look at me as a celebrity first—there are a lot of people up here that know me; I give them a card, they say, 'Yeah, I know you—you one of my favorite players,' that type of deal, so now I'm not just black, I'm a black celebrity, so it's a bit different.

"You look at a lot of white families—and I'm not saying it's their fault—but the majority—not the majority, but a lot of white families, say, they have an inheritance, or their family take care of them, as far as, like, they have their own business and different things, which the black families don't have. You look at most blacks that accomplished anything, they usually accomplished it on their own, they didn't have a family that had a business or something—you may hear about it every now and then, but mostly it's the white kids that have that. So they have a stable foundation, they have a background, you know, if they want to go to college, they can go. We have this one kid at the dealership, he's nineteen years old, his family has money—I won't say they're filthy rich, but they're comfortable, and he can go to college. His father bought him a 300 ZX, he just bought him a '93 and he drives around there, you know. He signed a contract—I couldn't imagine, it just tickled me, I just thought you'd never find that in a black family—he signed a contract with his own parents before he moved out of the house, saying that he would get pay for his groceries, they pay half his rent, and they give him an allowance of two hundred dollars a week, or something like that. And I said, well he's got it made; he was in a police academy for a while, but I think he had a problem with dizziness or something, and he had to drop out of that. So now, here's a kid, he can go to school, he can do anything he wants, and he wants to stand out there and sell cars. But I'm saying, just having that opportunity—that's what I want to do for myself. I don't want—you know, I took football for granted, as far as putting away money and stuff. The average football player doesn't make that much money. You have the superstars like Lawrence Taylor and other guys that make the serious money, and then they gonna be like seventh, eight round that's making maybe fifty to seventy-five thousand first couple of years, maybe a hundred and twenty-five; that's great money, but what if something happens to him, if he's injured, what's going to happen then? I had some money saved up but playing in the League I wasn't really a superstar, you know, I played and I started, but I wasn't a first-rounder, I didn't get a big sign-up bonus up front. And I took the money that I did get and I went in with this guy and opened a club, and the club fell through and I lost a lot of money. And then, my final year, I was traded to the Colts and after that I was cut, and the money kind of disappeared before I had a chance to rebuild it; you know, I would like to get something stable not for me, but for my kids, you know, be able to get them things, buy that computer for her, stuff I didn't have when I was a kid. I'd like to pretty much give them everything they need to have a comfortable childhood and then at least have—you know, their mom, she works and she takes care of them, she does a real good job with them, instills values in them, and so far everything is working, but it's just the environment they're in—I wish they could live somewhere up here like this. I think about bringing them up here, but I don't think it would work. Stuff happens around here too, but it's just a lot slower, you get to be a kid. There, in Miami, you grow up way too fast, you hear and you see things kids up here don't see. I grew up in a rough neighborhood. When my mom was married, we lived in a nice neighborhood, when my mom got divorced, we moved. My mom kept me out of trouble, off the streets, with sports. Mmhmm. And a hard right," said Orson ruefully. "For me, if I didn't have sports, I'd probably be in jail somewhere, if I was growing up as a kid. I mean . . . I mean when I was younger, if my baseball game got rained out, I wanted to cry, I would be disappointed, even though we're going to make it up, but I was so geared up to play that day, you know, and practice was fun and then you look forward to the games, 'cos you got to play other teams and you know, compete—that's what I lived for, baseball, when I was little, being able to compete and play. I wish I could go back there sometimes, you know, to where you don't have any cares in the world; when you're a kid you say I wish I was grown enough to get out on my own, but when you get out there, you know, it's shocking.

"I tell you one thing, being out there and being on the job market and looking for work and, you know, it said 'Experience necessary.' " Orson ran his finger down the table, as if running down the column of a newspaper. " 'Experience, experience, experience, experience,' and you go apply for a job and they find out that you played N.F.L. ball and they say—'Well, this little bit of money here isn't going to interest him,' so they don't hire you. So I felt real lucky to be able to get up here and get a job, and know I have the capability where if things don't work out here, I can go to another dealer shop. I'll have the experience. Right now it's the slow part of the year for selling cars, but January picks back up, and then as it gets hot this store here really picks up. So I'll be able to do some things with that and see what happens.

"I was two years at Florida State—'81 and '82; then '83 I didn't do anything, after I was kicked out. 'Eighty-four and '85 and until I came out in '86, I was in West Virginia, Salem, West Virginia. If I would have stayed at Florida State, I would probably have been a first-rounder. I would probably still be playing in the N.F.L. now. I know I would have some money. If I had been drafted higher—well, I would have money—when you're first round, they got a lot of money invested in you; you give a guy a million dollars, a million five, just to sign his name on a piece of paper saying that 'I am now the property of the Denver Broncos.' Then you're going to get second chances, you gonna get opportunities, they're going to look out for you because they have a lot of money invested in you. A sixth-round player, you know, it's either—if they can get some years out of you and save some money, they do it, then when they feel that you're going to cost them some money, they ship you somewhere else. And everybody doesn't fit into everybody's program; I found that out when I was with the Colts. The front office ran the team when I was there, I was seeing a lot of chaos and it just wasn't a good program, you know. A guy can be somewhere with a team and be the best player on the team and for some reason they cannot fit him into their scheme of playing, their type of game, and he can go somewhere else and can build back up for a year or two and sometimes he gets in there and becomes a star.

"I feel like right now my life would be different if I would have stayed at Florida State, if I had done the things I was supposed to do, 'cos one of the coaches, he tried to tell me; he sat me down one day and he said, 'Man, they're trying to get rid of you; they don't want you here because you're playing baseball, and they just looking for a reason to kick you out,' and he said, 'Don't give them a reason,' he said, 'I'll give you fair warning, because I like you as a person, and I like you as a ballplayer'; and he said 'Next year you can be an all-American, and the year after you're a senior; you can get drafted higher.' He said, 'You got things to look for, you can't just go by all that's happening now.' But then, it was too late then, you know, I was on academic probation, I needed to make a 3.0 to stay in school, and it was just—it didn't happen, you know, it just . . . you know, the talk came a little too late, it just kind of happened all so fast, and I think my life would be different; I think I'd still be playing; you know, there ain't no telling what I'd have; a million dollars is a lot of money, just to have up front, and that's not talking about your salary, and that's what I would have been looking at if I'd have stayed at Florida State, barring injuries."

Our interview had ended, and Orson stood up, saying he had to get the barbecue under way. His nephew and niece had come home from school while we had been talking and had been busy playing a video game in the den. The nephew, the studious one, now emerged in time to overhear his uncle's plans: "*You're* cooking?" he asked incredulously.

"I've cooked before," said Orson, defiantly looking down at him from six feet five inches above the ground. The good son, back where he thought he would not be, in his mother's house.

Before I left, Orson vanished ponderously down the hall to his room, returning with three football trading cards, each with a picture of Orson Mobley on the field—two in brawling action, one standing contemplatively with his helmet off. On the back of the card, I read:

ORSON MOBLEY
Denver Broncos, Tight End

HT: 6'5"   WT: 259   COLLEGE: SALEM
DRFT: BRONCOS #6-1986   ACQ: VIA DRAFT
BORN: 3-4-63, BROOKSVILLE, FLORIDA
HOME: MIAMI, FLORIDA

Orson was named the Broncos' Player of the Game after having 6 Receptions for 55 Yds. vs. Browns, 11-13-88. He won All-West Virginia Conference honors at Salem.

Carefully, he signed each card "O. Mobley, #89", just as he must do for his customers at the dealership.

"At least you have something to remember," he said, handing them to me.

JESSIE

"How Much I Miss Home," by Jessie Hester; "How Much I Miss Home Cooking," by Jessie Hester—all of Jessie's essays were variations of the same essential theme. "How Much I Miss My Room at Home (My room at home is sunflower yellow. My mother made me matching curtains and a spread. . . .)."

At the end of every semester, the athletes had to clean their apartments and pass an inspection before they were allowed to leave Tallahassee and go home.

"Jessie," the other players used to tease. "Did you hear about what happened to Ricky last semester? They found one pin—*one pin*—lying on his carpet, and they wouldn't let him leave."

Similarly, at the last tutorial session of the first semester, the players reported to me that Jessie, who had been packed and ready to go for a week, was even now, as they spoke, sitting on the edge of his bed "like this"—bolt upright, hands clasped in lap, legs neatly together—scared to move and mess anything up.

Jessie could take any amount of teasing because he was squarely, confidently, grounded in himself. Looking at him, one saw the product of a lifetime of adoring women—sisters, mother, girlfriends—who had all catered to his charm. He was extremely good-looking, with the even, clean-cut features of a matinee idol, although his perfect smile and twinkling eyes made him "cute" more than handsome; his were the playful, unthreatening good looks of a best friend's older brother. Jessie had been blessed with many gifts. He was one of the standout freshman talents on the team, and with Billy Allen and quarterback Mike Rendina got the most preseason press. He had clocked the fastest sprint times on the squad—4.48 seconds for forty yards and, even more impressive, 9.6 for one hundred yards.

I never realized at the time that he had star potential. I hadn't been around Tallahassee to read the preseason publicity, and he didn't really come into his own until after I had gone. Also, my impression of him based only upon our tutorial sessions was that he was, as the other players used to say, too "careful of his ownself" to shine in the rough-and-tumble of a sport like football.

For instance: One winter evening immediately before we met for tutorials, the boosters held a Christmas party for the players (chiefly memorable, as far as I'm concerned, for the ineradicable image it left me of Orson Mobley and Pat Woolfork and other unlikely persons singing "Rudolph the Red-Nosed Reindeer" while holding helium-filled balloons). My group of players arrived in our classroom carrying leftover balloons and cookies. The cookies Jessie refused to eat, saying that he could feel the sugar "shoot up his jaw"—evidently, booster cookery, like everything else, failed to match what he was used to at home. But he couldn't resist joining the others in inhaling helium from the balloons, which gave their voices a high-pitched quack, like Donald Duck's. Some time after the helium supply had been exhausted and things were more or less back to normal, I became aware of the fact that Jessie was standing on his head in a corner of the room, bouncing up and down with his mouth open.

John Feagin, laughing, explained. "We told him that the gas could go to his brain, you know; that people *died* from doing what he just did. You know how careful Jessie is of his ownself."

Because of his charm and good humor, Jessie could get away with a lot of—usually innocent—mischief. In his impersonations of other people and renditions of the imaginary situations he placed them in he was without peer—sheer inspired brilliance. Again, with every performance of his, one could picture the audience he had grown up with at home; the squeals of indignant, appreciative laughter, with him, Jessie, at the inevitable center.

"No seriously," he would say, after asking some provocative question, "no now, I'm being serious," but his mock sober expression would begin to slip, his eyes to dance, and soon he would be openly in laughter. I sensed that his humor had always been if not a weapon, for he was not a hard enough person to require one, then an old ally on which he was accustomed to draw to defuse uncomfortable situations. He indulged in humor for humor's sake—but he also understood the saving power of laughter.

Jessie's papers were the most difficult to grade, because in unconventional ways his diction was often poetic.

"As the sun rose, so do we," he wrote about beginning the day at a summer camp. Was this lyrical, effective line really wrong? In figures of spoken as well as written speech, and most particularly in his little skits of other people, one caught glimpses of his whimsical but perceptive imagination. Whether he wrote or acted out his imaginings, he brought to his audience a vivid re-creation of the "picture" in his own mind.

Three years after I left Tallahassee, my mother wrote to me in Africa that Jessie Hester had been drafted to the L.A. Raiders in the first round. A local television station had been in his dorm room when he received the call, and at that moment he was the toast of Tallahassee. Jessie had always given the impression that things came easily to him, and one was led to believe that fate, as well as he, was careful of his ownself. Now, he had been drafted higher than any other player of his year.

Although I wasn't aware of his football skills at the time I worked with him, I had no doubt that he was a rare and first-class athlete. One night in study hall, Greg Allen had nonchalantly executed a standing back flip. I had expressed amazement, and Jessie, giving me a meaningful "you wait and see" glance, had put down his books and bounding a few steps down the gym executed a back handspring followed by a high-flying layout back flip; his ownself was not going to be upstaged. I thought of my own feeble years on a gymnastic team, which incidentally had produced nationally ranked competitors. No one there, with all their careful warm-ups, mental preparation, years of practice, had ever performed this stunt any better than the six-foot man who had just walked out of the cafeteria full of dinner at the end of a day of football practice, dressed, moreover, in tight jeans. The height, the easy form—his back flip had been near perfect.

"Yeah, Jessie does all those kind of things," I remember John Feagin telling me. Years afterward, when I came to look Jessie up again, I recalled this incident and asked him if he could have excelled at other sports. His eyes had twinkled with his old, almost conspiratorial mischievousness.

"Anything," he said. No need for false modesty. What he spoke was only the truth.

When it came time to try to find Jessie, the first place I turned to was Belle Glade. Through information, I learned that his mother at least was still a resident there but was reachable only through an unlisted number. I then tried the Colts, for whom I knew Jessie was still playing. Although I got quickly through to the main office, and then the media relations department, it took many months before I actually got hold of Jessie Hester. When I first started calling, the team had just arrived in Indianapolis for preseason training camp, and my attempts to schedule an interview afforded me a narrow but educational glimpse of the life of a professional football player. Apparently, the players had only one free day a week, which most of them used to rest. I told the media relations representative that I would be happy to meet

Jessie in the evening if this would be more convenient, but was told that the evenings were devoted to studying films and videos. In other words, Jessie's schedule appeared to be much as it had been at Florida State; I vividly recalled the time-allocation sheets that the players there had been given, with an hour of "leisure time" generally budgeted once a day, somewhere in the evening.

After the preseason, of course, came the season; and after the season was over, I received a phone call from the Colts office telling me that due to the N.F.L.'s mandatory budget cap, the Colts had been forced to make some cuts and Jessie had been let go. Now his time would be taken up traveling to audition and interview with other teams. My first overtures to meet with Jessie had taken place in August of 1993, and it was nearly Easter of 1994 before I succeeded in seeing him, at his home in West Palm Beach.

Jessie's home was in a new upmarket housing estate less than half an hour's drive from the West Palm Beach airport. The entire southern and even central sections of Florida are parts of the state I have spent a lifetime avoiding, and en route to his home I felt a wave of nostalgia for the other Florida I knew—the rugged, knotty, unmistakably ancient oaks, the prehistoric clumps of frazzled moss, the tangle of unmanageable lianas and vines and foliage; there was no allowance for such uncouth and anciently vested elements here. The entire landscape I now passed through was not groomed so much as remade, entirely artificial, created like a convenience store solely to cater to the banal desires of its most recent settlers.

Passing through the portals that fronted the estate, I came to a quiet inlet off the through road, a small court shared by two houses. In the back of one, a group of children could be seen and heard playing in a screened-off swimming pool; outside the other was a red Isuzu Trooper and a fire-engine-red Mercedes convertible. No sign of life at all could be seen within, but when I knocked on the door it was immediately opened by Jessie himself. He was both the same and not the same as I had remembered. The same smile and eyes, but thicker in the neck and not so boyish. Although he looked extremely fit and trim, it was the lean, carefully maintained fitness of an older man, not the silky litheness of an eighteen-year-old natural athlete. He was dressed very simply in jean shorts and a T-shirt, with a discreet rope of gold glinting underneath. Shining with mesmerizing brightness from his wrist, however, was a gleaming diamond-studded Rolex.

"Yeah, come on in," said Jessie easily. There were no lights on inside, and it was hard to tell where he had been sitting. On entering the house, I was reminded of the homes of minor dignitaries I had seen in small African nations—the official residence of a U.S.A.I.D. director, perhaps—being at the same time both grandiose and basic. One floor under a flat Florida roof, an entrance room and dining room that you sensed were less used than the enormous kitchen with its wraparound counter facing a wall-size film screen. Minimal hotel-lobby furniture, with the most heavily decorated room being the game room, which was covered with trophies and plaques mostly emblazoned with the insignia of the Colts and F.S.U. Big rooms sparsely furnished and dimly lit—perhaps to counteract the outside glare of heat with the illusion of shadowy coolness. A swimming pool and screened porch lay beyond the game room. Jessie said that he had been living here for one and a half years; I would have guessed only a few months. Perhaps the realities of his schedule—five months of the year spent in Indianapolis—made the house less than wholeheartedly lived in; perhaps, as I wondered later, it was because his heart really did lie some miles from here, back home in Belle Glade.

"Do you remember what you used to write your essays about?" I asked him at one point in the interview, as we sat together at the big counter, like two patrons of an abandoned drugstore soda fountain.

"It was most probably about home," he replied, without losing a beat.

Remarkably, Jessie had returned to F.S.U. after his first season in the pros to finish his degree.

"Yeah," he said, "after I was drafted and played a year in the N.F.L., I just, you know, decided to go back, simply 'cos it's something that *I* wanted to do, you know, and it wasn't that long a term—I needed another semester; plus when I went off to college that was something that my mom asked me and I promised her that I would do.

"I actually could have finished my degree that same semester that I got drafted, but I was too caught up in the hype of getting drafted, and I had to drop a couple of classes and therefore I didn't graduate; I was just too caught up, too involved with what was about to happen as far as the draft that I couldn't concentrate on school, and I felt instead of, you know, flunking any classes, I better just drop them and just come back after the season is over and finish up; so once it was over and I had basically all the time and not have to worry about going to practice, you know, it give you a whole lot more time to concentrate on books.

"I was a social science major. At first, basically, I wanted to get into the business field, but more and more I got into it, it was too time-consuming for myself and I was still, you know"—he paused, the grown-up seriousness slipping from his face—"the kinda outgoing type—wanted to get out there and party a little bit, so it kind of took away from my time and at that point I wasn't sure enough to set aside the partying part of it. I felt if I'm going to get a degree, I've got to find something I like doing, and the social science is so versatile, as far as you can do most anything with it, you know, cover so many different fields, I thought I'd best go that route. 'Cos there's a political science part in it, you know, and social work—I could probably do that right now, that type of job, so like I say, there are a number of things that it can mix with; I may need a little bit more schooling now, a little bit more, but that's not too frightening, I can go and do that.

"How was I recruited to F.S.U.? Coach Billy Sexton came down, and"—Jessie paused to laugh—"it was a madhouse. It was crazy. I basically had to stay over to my grandmother's house, you know, because basically every day people from, I guess Notre Dame, Michigan, Ohio State—you name the school, they were basically at my mom's door trying to talk to me, trying to persuade her as well, so I either had to stay at my grandmom's or my girlfriend's house, you know, just to get a little peace and quiet. 'Cos at that point I just—I wanted to make this decision for myself, you know, basically not be influenced by I guess the prestige of the school and the influence of my mom—and basically what it wounded down to was me being influenced by my mother. 'Cos I decided, OK, I want to go to the University of Pittsburgh; I decided I wanted to go there. A guy came down for me to sign the letter and, you know, I had started to sign and I just looked at my mom for some odd reason and I could see she wasn't happy at all. Right, so I called her in the bathroom; 'OK, what's wrong with you?' " Jessie asked, falling into his old habit of enacting scenarios and mimicking first himself, then his mother. " 'Like baby, I don't want you to go up there, it's too far, it's too cold.' " Jessie drew a big sigh. "All right. I came back out, told the guy, 'Well my mom, she's not happy, and you know, and I can't do it right now because she's not happy,' so I said, 'I'll call you next week and let you know,' and then Coach Bowden called on the phone: 'Jessie, we need to know what your plans are, what you going to do, we need to know that right now,' you know, 'we got big plans for you.' I said, 'All right Coach, I'll call you back and let you know within a day or two.' So I pondered about it and I thought well, the University of Miami was too close, about an hour away, so I said no, that's just too close to go and I'm not going to bother with the University of Miami, although I liked their school quite a bit; and Gainesville was kind of too much like home—there was a whole lot of people I knew from high school that went there, plus the school was kind of too big for me basically, it was too spreaded out. And I thought about Florida

State University, how it was, you know, a kind of big campus but compacted together, everything was basically in walking distance. After, you know, coming from a small place like Belle Glade, I guess I could feel at home here. And then that's basically what I decided on. I wanted my first year to go well. I figured if I was somewhere not comfortable, having to get on some complicated bus schedule far as having to catch this bus to go 'cross town to come back—no. 'Cos I knew that the freshman year was probably going to go be the hardest year, just trying to get adjusted as far as football, plus academics, so I figure that was the deciding factor right there for me.

"As far as classes, I always felt like everything basically was going to be on my shoulders. You know, if I was lazy, if I flunked out it was going to be because *I* flunked out, it wasn't because of the school was too hard, or too easy or too whatever; it was going to be because of what effort I put into it. Like when I first walked into the classroom I just—the number of peoples, you know like—whhoooe. You know what I'm saying? One class—I think it was a biology class—that class had to have more students in that one particular class than in my whole graduating class in high school, so you know it was a complete shock just to see that. I guess that knowing that the professor definitely didn't know faces and when he graded stuff it was basically by social security number, you know—you here, you're a number and you just got to take the most out of it while you're here because this guy, he basically isn't going to have time for you simply because that's three, four hundred students there; he can't just say, 'Well, Jessie, you need help,' no, he can't do that, so basically you got to sit and watch and see what's going on and take advantage of the tutoring sessions that they have up there at Florida State as well. So all that stuff played a vital part of getting me to the point of that first year, of getting acclimatized to college life—what they call the 'athletic student' quote unquote type deal at Florida State.

"Yeah, I remember things from some classes. I had one biology class—I thought that was something that I'll always—like I go outside with my little boy watching things, you know, and the meteorology class as well, that was quite interesting; and the English class that we did all that Greek mythology stuff—there were definitely a couple of classes that stuck in my mind; the social science deal, that I got the degree in, you know, to see how things develop in this country. So I had quite a few classes that stick out in my head.

"I can't really say whether the class or the teacher made a difference; I guess it was really just something that interested me; I can't say why it did or why it didn't, it just did. Especially, like I say, the meteorology class. The people just start talking about the wind direction and you can tell which way the front is coming because of the wind and all of this type stuff, and when the dew's on the ground that chances are it may not rain. Once you hear it, it get interesting; you are like whooove. It was interesting to me, I guess, and it just captured me and I just stayed with it, basically. And that Greek mythology stuff, that was something that I always liked, even in high school, so that was just something that helped me. But I can't say as far as a teacher—I came back and basically I can't name a teacher for you, I cannot name a teacher; and in high school there ain't too many teachers I can name as well.

"I don't think I got special treatment in high school, as far as being an athlete. Naw, I really didn't, simply because the school that I go to, there's a hundred guys like me—really, seriously, seriously. Yeah, yeah, you got like two or three guys coming out of there this year, probably two or three of the best guys in high school. I don't know why. I can't answer, because I don't know. But you know, like for the area itself, we had some tremendous talent come up out of that place.

"I felt like through our high school, that's when I had adequate English classes, English studies, to prepare me well enough—but I guess not, because once you got up there to college without certain skills that you needed to perform, then it showed. I can't quote unquote answer that one, because I actually feel, I truly, honestly feel that throughout the school system as far as coming up through high school I was adequately prepared, you know, had enough English subjects and just prepared good enough to do well in school; then once you get there, you realize what's required and you know then, you realize that it wasn't enough.

"What kind of English did we do in high school? Well . . ." There was a long silence. "I'm trying to think what—now, it wasn't writing, it couldn't have been writing, it was mostly reading, it was probably mostly reading and mostly spelling, mostly like that. I didn't write little short papers like that, not that I can recall. I could be kind of crossed up on high school and college right now, I know there was five-hundred-, two-hundred-fifty- to five-hundred-word essays in college, if I'm not mistaken; yes, there were—they had to be typed as well. So assume that's college. I don't think we had to do that in high school.

"Now? I read occasionally, I have a couple of little books, basically Terry McMillan, I read a lot of her stuff and you know, then this . . ." He mischievously reached across the counter and picked up the copy of a book of mine that I had brought for him. "No, I can read this—because it's not too *thick*; if it's not too thick, and then once I get into it, if it can hold me at the beginning, then I figure I can finish it.

"In college, the only time I read was basically when I had to study for something, that was basically the only time I read. When I was in high school, as far as reading like, you know, in an English class that we're doing a play, *Macbeth* or something, I might have a little part, a little line to read, but that was basically about it; but as far as actual reading no, I didn't do it. Even like at home, and I see like Mom or my brothers and sisters, all of them, they read, you know, they was, quote, fine at it, but for me, that was just something I don't do. Right now, like you say, 'How are you doing with your kid?' I always try to stress if *I* don't read to him, if he don't read to me, usually my fiancée read to him, or he read to her, so I want to try to at least get him into the framework at an early age of liking it.

"My mom basically raised us on her own, yeah, basically—I mean, my grandmother and my grandfather they lived kinda around the corner. Six, there were six of us. Just two went on to college, my older brother and myself. My sisters"—Jessie laughed, looking at me with an expression of exaggerated meaningfulness—"they got with the guys and stayed around home, so to speak, but they all finished high school. It was what you call a nice tight-knit family and"—he stopped suddenly, looking down at the counter—"uh . . . uh, you know, it will be tough . . . I can't imagine, I just can't imagine it, I won't even think about it. You don't even think about it.

"My mom was concerned as far as the grades that was brought home from high school; she basically didn't have time maybe to go to school and see what they were actually teaching us, you know, simply because she had to go to work and when she get home from work, she was tired and she had to do cooking and stuff like that, and the cleaning; so when we brought home the report cards and, you know, it didn't reflect like what she felt they should reflect, we kind of paid for it, so to speak. She out there working hard, slaving, basically, to keep us at school and we in school and ain't learning nothing, you know, she won't go for that basically. Like I remember at great length, in fourth grade, that was a turning point for me, in the fourth grade, not necessarily as far as grades but as far as absences; you know, I'm going to be in school if there is going to be a test. I show up for the test—just about in any class I know enough to pass, just by being in class, so I can do that, you know, I did all right. But this particular time she looked down and the absences was—they had to be well over close to about thirty days; I was skipping with a couple of my buddies—ssssss." Jessie drew his breath, pausing over a private memory, then jumped ahead. "So like I say, from that point on . . ."

"What did she do?"

As if still wincing, Jessie looked at me cautiously sideways, talking out of the corner of his mouth.

"Took a branch of the tree . . . and after—I will never forget that, never forget. And from that point on, if I wasn't sick, I never missed a day of school. Never missed a day of school. I always joke when I tell her that, I say 'Jeez, Mom, you probably go to jail. You go to jail back in those days.' And I tell my little boy, I say 'Man, don't try, because she's just a changed woman right now, she's a changed woman, this woman here was something else, coming up.' I can see that day just as vivid as—sshhh. That had to be the turning point. But if she didn't care, I'd probably still be skipping. She's out working hard to make sure that we got clothes on our backs and a roof over our head and food to eat and the way that we show our appreciation is to do stuff like that.

"Where did she work? Basically you name it, she did it. It's from the—what they call that vegetable?—out in the fields; from the fields, to the hotels to—you name it, she did it. Once I got up in high school, she got a manager job at a hotel far as the cleaning personnel; she was the head of the cleaning thing in the hotel and she stayed in that for a while and I was glad to see her in that because it wasn't a physically, you know, too demanding type of job. I was glad to see her going in and she liked it and it paid well, and she was quote unquote boss over, she had at least about twenty workers I guess, people that was underneath her, and I told her I was proud of her for having manager skills and she had to do paperwork, keep the inventories, and do stuff like that, and it help her grow as far as who she is today, and that was good to see.

"I try to get over in Belle Glade as much as I can, to the schools, so the kids can see me, and not quote unquote be a TV figure all the time; lots of them just see me on TV and just know I'm from Belle Glade; but if they actually see me and feel like they can come up and talk to me anytime they want to talk to me, that I am actually just like they are, then they can realize, 'Hey, I can do it as well,' you know what I'm saying? But I still have to try to talk to them that there's more you have to do, there's always more; I mean everyone can probably be athletic, but today you have to have a lot more to probably get yourself a chance, to allow yourself the chance; if you can get out of high school now you can go to college—but now you got to be able to at least stay in college for two years, so if you can do that, now you're giving yourself a chance; but if you can't do that, you have no chance."

"Don't they ever see a chance in their books?" I asked. "Don't they ever think books could be the way out?"

Jessie closed his eyes and shook his head.

"They don't see it. They hear it, trust me, they hear it, they hear it all the time, but for some odd reason they cannot see it. I don't know what can link it, for it to get that connection to make them realize that they can be successful in something else, you know. It may be art, it may be writing, whatever it may be, but for some odd reason, they can't—they cannot make the connection, and why, I do not know. Maybe they don't see enough of those type of professions in the community; mostly all they see that's basically a success in their eyes are drug dealers. That's mostly what the guys see, those type of people that are mostly flashy anyways, 'cos the younger guys, that's what they want to be, flashy, and they want to get that quick money right away. I think it's got to be in the community, it's got to be where they can see these other people in the community. Because they know, they know that there are some successful black professionals out there, but they may think that they came from the quote unquote Huxtable-type family, see, they figure they came from those type of families, and they got to realize that it's not like that, you know, it's not like that. But I think it's in the community, they got to see it in the community, then when their mom say something like 'I went to school with him'—that's what I like to hear the most, right there, 'Hey I went to school with him.' And the kids say, 'You did?' And now they know, you know, exactly where he did come up. But I try to, I guess, get to the reality of it, you know, 'Guys, trust me, it can happen for you,' and it hurts, it really hurts that you know a lot of them probably going to not make it, 'cos you know what lies ahead for a lot of them, if they don't make their turnaround."

I asked him if his visits to the school were part of a community program. "No, I do this on my own, it's on my own. Basically, it's the simple fact that I feel like I owed it, you know, to the community, being the first quote unquote guy to leave out of there on a professional level as far as football, and I know what type of area it is as far as athletics, you know, and knowing the ramifications it can have as far as guys being ignorant to the fact of going into a certain situation blind, going to college; so I figured, I at least can add a little something and at least give them a little insight on what to expect and hopefully help them out. Like I said, after I left, Ray McDonald, he came up in a couple of years, John Ford, Rhondy Weston, Louis Oliver, Jimmy Spencer—I mean you got two other guys probably gonna come out in the next two or three years, you got these two guys coming out of high school that's awesome; hopefully, those guys will come back as well and do it—if they could come back as well and do the same thing, it may not get them all, but as long as you get a few, you know.

"The kids mostly want to know about the pros, basically that's what they want to know about. They don't want to know about how it was when I came up; but when I speak to them, I'm always telling them, 'cos I know they not going to ask. Mostly they ask me, you know, 'Are you married, got any kids, how much money you make?' You know, 'Do you know that player, do you know that player?'—they go through stuff like that. That's it, that's it. I tell 'em, I say for all the Sundays, all of that final picture of what a pro ballplayer is, I say, you don't know what he has to go through for that whole week, 'cos it's tough. The training camp just to make the team, it's tough.

"With the women, the basic thing that I try to say to them is, you know, 'Don't let these little boys get you pregnant, hold you back; you know, once you get pregnant, it's kind of hard for you to get away, see.' I guess it's hard if they can't see beyond where they are. You know, if their mom or dad are not saying anything positive to them, you know, they can't see beyond where they are. I always try to give them hope, I always try to give them hope, I always try to say, 'Allow yourself the chance. Allow yourself the chance.' Chance to do what I don't know, but at least allow yourself the chance. I mean, if you have a child, it's going to be harder for you, because now you got to provide for a little child—and it's harder for the child too. I always press 'em: 'Now, if you want to *meet* a guy like me, quote unquote, if you want to meet a person like me, a professional, a doctor, a lawyer, see what I'm saying? If you want to meet a guy like me, there are plenty of guys like me in college. Puh-lenty of them—doctors, lawyers, engineers, I mean plenty of them.' I say, 'Your mom may not have gone to school—you know why? Maybe 'cos she had you. That's probably why she didn't go.' I'll say, 'You ask her—ask her; she probably didn't go because she had maybe to take care of you or maybe if you had an older brother or sister or somebody, that's probably where it started from. But you ain't got to be that way, you don't have to be that way. You young, you're about fourteen, fifteen years, you young. I ain't telling you not to have fun, I'm not telling you that, because I know how I was, I wanted to have fun as well; but if you feel like you got to have sex, you know what I mean? There's all types of birth control, all types.' I can see the ones that I'm getting to; the ones that I'm getting to, they're basically the ones that maybe already made a decision to do that, and the ones that don't want to, you know, you can see them kinda shying away, are the ones that know that they are already doing this, and they like what they're doing, and they don't want to give it up. So I can look at them, and those I really try to stare down. The girls, you think they're easier to reach because they're not as loud and rowdy as most of the boys, yeah, you would think that you getting to them. The girls invariably probably go to college a whole lot more than the guys, yeah, over there the girls they go and graduate; I'm proud of those girls there. I mean that would be interesting to find out what the ratio to that is; I'm willing to bet it's probably four or five to one, it could be even higher. I think the girls realize that school is the way for them, and they do allow, seeing mostly the opportunity that the guys have and probably not taking advantage of it; 'cos you hear all the girls all say, all the time, 'I wish I could play football,' you understand? Because they realize, you know—you can hear the girls saying that, but the guys, they take it for granted, so to speak, they 'OK, I can do it and I know I can get out of here with it.' But that all you got to trust, you understand? God gave you the ability to play the sport, but you going to have"—Jessie laughed—"you going to last about ten years if you're lucky; if you can get ten years out of it, you're lucky, and then what you going to do after that? If you ain't smart enough to hold on to your money, or do a little something wisely with your money, you get out of the game and you basically ain't got no money to take care of yourself, whatch you going to do? But the guys, you can tell them, but they can't take it; it ain't going in, it's not registering, for some reason.

"I myself, I never was quote unquote flashy. You know, I didn't need a whole lot, I think, for me to live, you know, I wasn't quote unquote flashy. This is a flashy watch," he said, fingering it with something approaching disdain. "But I didn't buy this—my *money* bought it, but it wasn't nothing that I go in the store and do myself. You know, my fiancée, she thought that I would like it and she, she got it, so to speak, I didn't. I told her, you know, I don't gripe about stuff like that but"—Jessie's eyes narrowed—"don't do it again." He laughed. " 'We can always take it back!!' " he said, imitating his fiancée. " 'No, no, that's fine, but just don't, don't, don't spend money like this on a watch like that.' It's the second time having it on. And the only way I'm wearing it is 'cos I hate just leaving it in the house; I have to keep it with me and I got change, coins in my pocket and they be scratching it up and I say I better wear it and maybe keep it a little safer that way. But like I say, I'm not that flashy, I feel I don't really need a whole bunch of money to live off; I want to live comfortably, that's basically about it, and I have—about the only hangup I have probably is for cars—buy myself a fancy car—but I can fight myself and hold back on that as well.

"Right now, I got my little boy in private school and knowing, you know, the on-hand experience that he can get from the teachers at an early age, and then once he likes school and just get in good study habits, then basically I think I can kind of take him out of it and just let him go from there and just watch him and see. You know, the determining factor of the matter is what you're getting out of high school as far as at least the *willingness* to learn, because I figure once you get to college and you can see what's going on, you may be a step behind, but that don't mean that you can't catch up. But I think that as long as they get that at the high school, the willingness to learn—that's what I had, at least the willingness to learn. I mean I wasn't, I guess, well prepared to the point where some schools are, but I had the desire, so to speak, I had the desire to learn and I wanted to learn.

"My son is athletic." Jessie smiled. "I am going to just let him be, so to speak, letting him choose to do what he want to do, and the thing for me is I want him to be academically inclined; basically, basically I want him to do what he want academically. For me personally, I feel that athletic-wise, you know, I think he's going to be blessed as well, basically, to do what he want as well, youmsaying? But I told him, 'I want you to be better than your daddy.' He may think I'm talking better as far as athletic-wise at this point, but I'm talking overall, youmsaying? 'So if you want to get that business degree that your daddy wanted to get, but your daddy felt like he had to, you know—didn't have the wits, I guess, enough, 'cos he did want to go out there and go to the little frat parties and whatnot—you know, you can be better than your daddy. And you may want to be a doctor or engineer,' youmsaying? I want him to go in the computer field—I'm going to mention it to him, I ain't going to force it to him, 'cos I feel like that's part of what society is going to be basically based on. He's seven. We are trying to get him to—he's brought home one C, but I told him, 'I ain't going to harp on that, but you know you can get that C up. If you feel like that's the best you can do in that class, you know, I can't question that, but you know within yourself if that's the best you can do. You can fool me, but you can't fool yourself'; but, yeah, he's an excellent student. He likes school—but he's kind of maybe like I was. See, what they call them when you see stuff backwards sort of? I was."

"Dyslexic? I didn't know that!"

"*I* knew it," said Jessie, "but I didn't tell nobody."

"But how could you have gone through my tutorial class and never bother to tell me that?" I asked indignantly. ("Caroline," he had said twelve years ago, "I could read this book every day of my life and I would not be through in two years.")

Jessie looked both amused and, uncharacteristically, shy.

"I . . . I . . . I was just mostly embarrassed about it. Not . . . not knowing, you know what I'm saying? how people would react to you about it. He's slightly, he's slightly, you know, he see letters, he may get letters mixed up, you know—"

"But when did you know this about yourself?" I asked, trying to get him back on track to himself.

"I always knew it."

"Did you know that other people didn't see words that way, the way you did?"

"No, no. Well, I don't know. Like I can't . . . I can't explain it, I can't explain it. About a couple of months ago I just, I guess he had to take a test or whatnot, and I told her, my fiancée, I said, 'I bet he come back slightly, probably, dyslexic.' She said, 'Why you say that?' I said, ' 'Cos I'm kinda.' She say, 'What?' She didn't know it either. And he came back and the teacher told her. He was, she said, he was kind of having problems reading things, right? And I told her I knew that's what it was. And that's exactly what it was. See, that's the same with—when I may read

something, I say, 'Oop, I didn't see that right.' I know myself I
didn't see that right, so I look back over there and I see the word.
It was like driving in the car with Mom, you know, looking at the
signs and stuff, look up see the sign: 'That doesn't say that.' You
look back at it, and you see what it actually says. I just thought
that I was reading too fast. That's what I kind of thought: 'Maybe
I'm reading too fast, trying to read too fast.' Then going from
word to word, and I see it be the same way. Yeah. So I think then
I have to just focus. I still do it today, but it's no problem. I figure I'm out of school and I'm not even trying to go get help for
it so . . . but he's definitely—*now* he better, he's better. He's just
reading like he should be, so that's good."

"What subjects do you want little Jessie to learn in school?" I
asked. "What subjects do you feel are necessary? Math, for instance—some people say that you only need enough math to be
able to count your money."

"No," said Jessie firmly, "I think math is tops; math, science,
and definitely reading and writing, English definitely. Basically I
think it helps you probably verbally to speak quite well, probably builds confidence as well, knowing that. Knowing how to
read, you know, just knowing how to talk, knowing mathematics, feeling that if you see something, any type of equation, whatever it may be, you feel comfortable doing it. I just think it build
character, I really do, I just think it build character, confidence
within a person, you see what I'm saying? That's something nobody can take from you as well, knowledge. I mean the Man up
above can take it from you, but that's it, nobody else can take it
from you, once you get knowledge, that's just in there. I always
heard that, you know, 'Never take it away from you.' I'm like,
'What . . . what do you mean by that?' Youmsaying? It took me
a while, but I know. Like they say, knowledge is the key. The person who is able to read, write, mathematics—yeah, you may be
able to count your money, that's fine, but someone that's smarter
than you is able to take your money, see, so that's the thing. If
you smart enough to be able to read, you know, you got contracts

in front of you, whatnot, like I got to go through, you know, the legal *herein*s and *therefore*s. I ain't no lawyer, so that's why I'm like, 'Well, I can read it, but the *herein*s and *therefore*s throwing me off,' so now I got to go pay somebody to tell me exactly what all these stipulations mean in this contract. So if you're wise enough to do all of that, you don't need nothing. Math, science, English," he said, rapping the counter with each word, "if you get those, you can't be stopped, I don't think.

"As far as these quote unquote ethnic curriculums, I want my son to know exactly what society going to be about. Basically, as far as I grew up, you know—naw, he ain't got to know about all that stuff, you know, naw. You know, I want—he need to know what basically black slogans and slang and all that stuff is. *I* know it—I grew up in it; I say, 'Why you got to *teach* me that? I *know* that.' Youmsaying? That's something that you're not going to have, when you going out for a job interview—they don't want to hear that. You see what I'm saying? Nobody want to hear that. So teach—I want him to know what it going to take for him to make it in society. *Today's* society, you understand? He should know all that stuff growing up, that's quote unquote ethnic, you know, what happened to us, the surroundings he's involved in, he *should* know that. But that ain't going to help in today's society, no. I want him to be the best he can possibly be."

"But would it have helped you to have learned about your African heritage?" I asked. "Would learning about African history help your son?"

"No." Jessie looked perplexed. "No. No. It's nice to know African history for your self-satisfaction, which is fine, youmsaying? But you don't have to make it like you're saying, a curriculum where they have to know this—no. No. The only history he need to know about is his family history, basically, that's what I feel. I mean, so . . . so—yes, he's an African American, and they may take him back that far if he want to go that far, I mean . . . I mean—listen, I can't go back to Africa, as far as tracing my roots. I go all the way to my gramps, and he's like, 'Son, I can't take you back that far either.' Youmsaying? He didn't ask his dad or his granddaddy, so he don't know. I say, 'Well, I'll stop with you then, I ain't going to dig no further. That's it.' So I tell him that's where it stops. Anytime I take him over there to see gramps there, well that's it right there. It's his greatgramp. This is it. African history—how is it going to help them get a job? How is it going to prepare me when I go to college? How is it? They got . . . they going to have this on one of my English essays I have to do? If it's going to help me that way, it should. Is my mathematics going to be basically be—I don't know what type of mathematics Africans using, but is that type of mathematics going to help me here? You know what I'm saying? Or is that, the language that they speak, going to help me while I'm here? No. No. No. Uhuh. No. No. Uhuh. I want my little fellow to learn all he can learn, the basic skills, reading, writing, mathematics, science. I think once he gets those down, I mean if he get to the point to where he can handle those with ease, he's there. He's there. He can basically pick and choose what he want to do from that point. He ain't going to be afraid of nothing as far as, 'I can't handle that,' like his dad, you knowmsaying? I didn't think I can handle being no doctor—I knew for a fact I couldn't be no doctor. But if he's like I say, well prepared in those three fields, he can be what he wants to be; and I'm going to make sure that he's well prepared in those three fields and he can have the lease to choose to be what he wants to be."

"What if, around about age thirteen, he starts coming round with friends that you can tell are going nowhere?"

"I told him, I ain't going to never pick his friends. I ain't going never pick his friends, but when he going to have a problem with me is if I ever find any drugs on him, ever, or alcohol." Jessie laughed. "I don't even want him to be social; thirteen, no, definitely no alcohol, no cigarettes, none of that, none of that. 'I ain't going to pick your friends, but if they influence you any type of way, you must be willing to go live with them. You must be willing to go live with them, because I am not going to have you in

my house. I'm not going to have it, youmsaying? I'm not going to
have it. I don't want to choose your friends, but if I feel like I'm
teaching you right, you shouldn't have these type of friends with
you anyway.' So, that's the thing. You know, I talk to him every
day. Every day, about you know, there ain't no waiting about
telling him about drugs, or a certain time I tell him about this or
this—naw. If he got anything, any type of question he want to ask
me about, anything that come out of his mouth, I tell him whatever I know about it. I'm saying, I don't want him to be, like I
say, dumbfounded about nothing, I don't want nobody to be
able to pull the wool over his eyes and try to fool him that this is
that which it's not. I can't—even today I never seen cocaine.
Never seen it. Most guys, they got to be knowing that I don't
drink or smoke, you know, a lot of time they stay away from me.
So that's it. I can remember being in the cars with my cousins
and friends and they got the weed going, and on and on like, 'Yo
man'; I'm, 'No man, no man, let me out.' I walked four miles
home. 'Get me out of here.'

"It's totally different, it's totally different than when I was in
high school, simply because you can see how the kids act towards
the teachers. See, we couldn't talk back because they had the
paddles in the school when I was in school, teachers was able
to"—Jessie tapped his palm—"put their ruler on your hand, or
go to the principal—they didn't actually put the paddle on your
behind. See nowadays, the kids know that the teachers can't hit
them and do anything to them, so they stand up and make faces,
yelling at them—yes, yes—and you constantly got to tell somebody to sit down and do that and do this, you can't even teach a
class, 'cos you got too much disruption going on in your class.
Plus, the girls maybe want to hit the teachers, or you got the guys
bigger than the teachers, so I mean, what can you do? It's rough.
It's just too rough. I mean, when we came up it wasn't that way.
There's just no control. You got to be able to at least control the
kids, at least have control of your classroom, at least, to give them
a chance, the teachers at least got to have control of their class-

room. You know, I hate to see them when they just tell a kid 'Get out'—what you did is just basically, you just told that kid basically that he ain't no good and there ain't no hope for you—just go, youmsaying? Like when I go to the schools, I see one getting suspended, and I be like, 'Boy, boy, boy.' There got to be a better solution. There got to be a better solution now, 'cos when they tell that little kid to walk out, and then once he flunk out and keep flunking out or whatever, he ain't going to give up. Now he gonna put on that ski mask and go stick somebody up, go rob somebody, or be selling the drugs for somebody, see, so that's his only solution basically for surviving—I know the kid ain't going to work, want to work a hard job, I know he's not going to do that, and the only jobs out there for him will be a hardworking job; he's not going to want to do that. So when they put them out the door, I'm looking at them—now could you be the kid that killed me? Look at me; you could be the kid right here that killed me, this guy right here, they're putting out this door. He see me one day thinking I got something on me, which I never carry nothing on me, but this kid may think I got something, want to rob me.

"That's why I guess I don't want, you know, to be having that watch. That what I try to tell *her*," said Jessie. "But she can't see that. She say," he lapsed into another of his imitations, " 'They don't know what the watch is made of.' 'Baby, that watch got diamonds, it shine, they don't got to know.' Yeah, that's what I tell her. 'You going to get caught up in the wrong place at the wrong time sometime, boy all right, all right. Maybe you grew in a time where you may not have seen what I have seen.'

"I remember my first year that I came back from the Raiders. It wasn't no real close friends of mine, but guys they rode by the yard, saying, 'Jessie—uh, you got some money, man? Get some gas and go down to Miami?' 'No, man,' you know, I'm trying to brush them, 'No man, I don't have nothing.' 'See, hey man—look!' 'Yeah?' I look. They had bought a little shotgun with their guns, right? So what's the little son of a bitch do? 'Man, we're fixing to go Miami, stick . . . stick a store up,' and I say, 'What? You-all going to go rob stuff? No man, I definitely can't give you no money, man. I'm sorry.' He said, 'Hey, you don't give us no money man, we gonna come back and shoot your momma house up.' I say, 'What?' I say, 'I tell you what. You all keep going, hit the block, go on, just go on turn the corner and when you come back, man, maybe some money outside the gate here.' I put five dollars out, five dollars outside the gate. That was it. I knew them; I ain't never knew none of them would be killers, but then again, I don't know—I knew they was rough guys, I knew they would have shoot you, I know that for a fact, so maybe they are killers, seewhatm saying? They were the same age I were; I grew up with them, I always seen them fighting and doing crazy stuff like that so I knew what type of people they were.

"I go around with the guys and if there's commotion going on, any type of commotion, loud talking, any type like that just irks me too much, I just got to go. It's kind of sad, it's kind of like it's taking a little something away from you, you know, where you just can't, just while you have a little leisure, sit around just laugh and joke with the guys; all of a sudden you look around you and for me, if I look around, I try to see the beer bottles and what type, whatever that stuff—a reed, a weefer—whatever that stuff called, they got that, once I see all that stuff, I know it ain't nothing but trouble, so I go. You know, I say hi to the guys, whatever, blah, blah, blah, and I go. 'Cos I think that's nothing but trouble, especially if any type of little heated argument going on, and I know all them probably got guns in their cars or they probably got them on them somewhere, so I say naw, a stray bullet don't know nobody, so I go.

"When I was drafted, it was a thrilling moment, and a great great time, you know, for me. In my senior year I realized I had a chance and I could really see it, and I knew that a lot—a lot of kids and a lot of guys that I have played with wanted this type of opportunity that I had, I knew it. And I seen, like I say, I seen guys come and go at Florida State, you know, a lot of them didn't get the opportunity, but I knew a lot of them was good ballplayers that should had the opportunity, you see, but now I'm given this opportunity. I knew Greg, Greg Allen, was going to be given that opportunity as well, I knew there was going to be a couple more players—Billy Allen—as well that same year, I knew there was going to be a couple more guys that was going to experience the same thing that I was experiencing as well, you know, so I was happy for them. The year that I was coming out, I could have predicted down the line that the guys like Hassan Jones and Cletis—I could have predicted that those guys would get drafted as well, you know, Jamie Dukes? I could have predicted that as well; but I'm just saying that I'm more so concerned about the guys I came in with, see. I knew by watching their progress—especially Greg's you know, I just knew that he and myself were definitely going to be drafted high. Billy and Darryl Gray—he got redshirted, he got hurt; I thought if Woolfork would've stayed in school I think he would have been a tremendous ballplayer—John Feagin as well, I though he had a chance to be an excellent ballplayer. Yeah, John was a good player, yeah, he could have been a good, good player. Lenny would have been OK, but I don't think he would have quite—he was a big guy, but for the position he was playing, he wasn't big enough, believe it or not." Jessie laughed almost wonderingly. "Believe it or not. Lenny was huge, but believe it.

"The pros can be rough. It depends, you know, you go out to practice twice a day, and it depends on what type of work that the team is doing that day; if it's good work, you may not be out there that long, but if the team having a bad practice, you could be out there a long time, you know, plus you may have to go against a defensive back, you know, and that guy may feel like hitting you that day and you may be getting some contact. Some days, you know, he may not feel like hitting you—I'm a receiver, a wide receiver, so that's where the guy may feel like he don't feel like getting hit today, so he decide he may not hit you, so it depends on the day. But overall it's always a lot of running for me 'cos I'm a receiver, so I always got to run around, so it's always constantly running, constantly running, always, so it's tiresome. It's constantly tiresome and, like I say, the physical part of it as far as getting knocked down, picked up, and knocked back down, so it's definitely what you call a physically demanding sport, and you got to like it to do it as well. I'm thirty-one; January I just turned thirty-one and—maybe two more, maybe this coming year and the following year, and I'll have to see how my body feel; as long as I'm able to run, you know, I feel like I'm able to stay out of harm's way, then I'll be fine. But as soon as I feel like I can't move as fast as I normally can, it's time to quit. It's time to quit, you know, you're kind of laying yourself out to get hurt, so I don't want to do that. I've been lucky, no, I've been lucky, I haven't had any serious injuries, I've been lucky. I've been lucky all around, I guess you could say.

"As far as what I'd do next, right now I'm mostly like I don't want to go to work for nobody, so basically I want to work for myself, I want to go into real estate. I want to go into real estate. At this particular moment I have a couple of, you know, ventures, as far as partnerships, as far as malls and office complexes, but I want to go mostly like into rental deals, you know like in apartment buildings and stuff like that where you get a monthly return and you can constantly see something coming in as far as a long-term deal. I want to do something in that field. I have a meat market too, that's a place where my mom—they're working in that, they call it the Family Meat Market, so all my family's working there. It was something that my brother thought of. Yeah, so that's basically what I want to do, 'cos I don't feel like I want to have to report to nobody and go to work. When I get up, that's the time I have to get up; that's how I want it. Once I get up, that's the time I get up, and then I have to go check on some property, or site I want to put something on—I go do that.

"No, I'm no longer with the Colts. I'm what you call a free agent, so I'm able to go to any team that I choose and that would like to have me as well, then we can work something out. Like I say, I've been traveling around to different teams, and I go up to Atlanta this Thursday. When I went out with the Rams, they wanted to see me run and catch the ball and stuff like that, but I went out to Cleveland and Cincinnati and they basically just talked and, you know, 'We like to have you' and stuff like that and now it's just a matter of them talking to my agent and just getting the finance, the money right. Once I go to Atlanta, that's going to be the final stop there, and I'm gonna just probably basically decide between those four teams as far as I want to go. They already made offers, but they all like to probably start low and my agent probably start high and then meet somewhere in the middle and then they go from there.

"A degree doesn't mean diddly-squat in the field, basically; I mean they may want to know whether the guy is smart, they may want to know that, because like a lot of time they say, 'The guy, he's not too smart,' and they get that from the quote unquote college coaches and they tell another the player is not so smart or whatever. Far as it can help you on the football field, as far as being able to comprehend, you know, certain things. Like the plays is just like learning; you looking at plays, you going to have to read it because it's written out, quote unquote this is what it is; and like totally simple mathematics, odd numbers to the left, even numbers to the right, so to speak, and you don't know that, you going to be lost in that sense as far as knowing which direction the play may go. Or they may call a route; does a three route mean this, or a four route mean that? See, so you gotta be able to at least read to be able to comprehend the signs to find out what's the language trying to tell you. And you have to have great memorization. Over at Florida State, you had to have Cadillac and Chevys and all this type stuff as plays, and so now you got to know what to do when they say Cadillac, Chevy, Ford, you understand? All them totally different plays. See, the number system basically can tell a person what to do if he knows what those numbers mean. If a guy calls it"—Jessie cupped his hand to his mouth—" 'Three fourty-four!' Right? He just told the outside receiver, tight end, and the other outside receiver exactly what to do. Then if the running back know the routes built in from those routes, he just told everybody what to do, and offensive line all know what their protection is. You cannot have time, you know, they don't have time to wait and just sit here and teach you this, you see what I'm saying? Therefore if you don't have time to learn on your own, then when the time in the heat of the battle, when you're competing against other guys who basically know what they're doing and you don't, you go out there and you doing wrong, they going to say, 'That guy is a dodo; he's dumb, he don't know what he's doing.' That's when those study habits come in again, you just got to be able to do that, you know, be able to carry over and take it out on the football field, what you learned in the classroom; *then* you learning, then you able to make the team and now they think that you're a smart guy and you know how to do the right thing, they can depend on you to *do* the right thing.

"I do know that I'm blessed and was guided to keep me out of trouble. The story my mom always told me, when I was real young, back—I don't remember. She say I was crossing the street and a truck was coming over and she was calling me back, and she said if I would have came back, I would probably have got killed and runned over, but she said I stopped and looked at her and kept going on across the street. I cannot say, I don't remember none of it, but stuff like that make me wonder; all the accidents, the things I see with kids that have been drowned and all the type of little accidents that take kids away and you always wonder what that person could have turned out to be. Every time, I mean every time I see something on television like that I always wonder—what that person could have turned out to be. So that's why I always look up and just know there was somebody up there that was guiding me, telling me, 'Jessie don't smoke that; Jessie, that person not a good person; Jessie . . .' You understand? Something, it had to be something, like I say, I just know the Man up above watching over me and protecting me, and I thank him for it.

"I don't go to church so much now. College and in the pros, I hadn't been doing it that much, and it kind of get me away from doing it that time, but I try to go, like I say, probably not as much as I should, but I know where my blessings come from, and I do get on my knees and pray; and if I'm not on my knees, if I'm in bed, I'm praying and thanking the Lord up above for blessing me. I do know where my blessings come from. To a great extent, I guess the overall picture of it, I guess you can say that I had a kind of charmed life, coming up. I say we certainly wasn't the richest peoples coming up, but we was happy and everybody loved each other and got along, and I never thought we was poor, or felt that; maybe we were, but I never felt that way 'cos like I say we always had food to eat, clothes on our back, a place to stay. And like I say, I go off to college and have a wonderful time in college, then get drafted into the pros, and here I am now. But, no I mean, I have to have rocky little spots, but it wasn't nothing to the point where I had to say should I shoot myself. I guess you could say it was quote unquote a little charmed life, and I'm going to try to take the best of this little ride that I'm having, and try to take it as far as I can till I run out of gas, you know, take this as far as I can, but, yeah, it been good."

Jessie's fiancée, Lena, hadn't returned home by the time I left, so I didn't meet her. They had met at F.S.U. and been together now for nine years. I gathered there was little chance of a wedding until Jessie was out of the pros and settled down in civilian life.

"Maybe another two years," he said lazily. "Coming up in a single-parent family, I don't want my son to, you know, if something happens, if we part, for him to think that's just the way it's supposed to be; two people get married, then divorced—that's it." Little Jessie had been at the neighbors' during my visit—it turned out that he was one of the children I had seen playing in the next-door pool when I arrived.

Jessie drove me to the airport—in the Isuzu, alas, not the Mercedes—and at the turnoff just beyond his housing estate, he paused for a moment.

"See that road?" he asked, pointing to the highway that ran past us. "If you follow that for twenty-seven miles, it will take you right to Belle Glade."

QUENT

Mad Dog; Q Dog; Quent Reed. Leaving the gym at the end of one study session, he had stood in the doorway, thrown back his head and howled like a hound; then, laughing, run down the stairs and out into the night, the rest of the group laughing and joshing with him from behind. His bullet-shaped head was closely shaven, and his eyes were set so that they looked in two different directions, one directly ahead, the other somewhere just off to the side. Although Quent was compactly built, unmistakably athletic, I could never imagine him playing football; his particular brand of raw, electric energy did not lend itself to containment in a uniformed, elaborately choreographed sport. Once he told me that he had left early in the day and on some urgent whim gone running out to a landmark I knew to be roughly seven miles away; "It was about twelve miles there and back," he said impassively. He had come back in time for practice, but had been tired, mainly because he hadn't eaten. I remember being more impressed by the stamina required, in this Florida heat, to make the run, than struck by the apparent meaninglessness of having made it in the first place, for this kind of urgent, unpremeditated rush of activity seemed to me entirely characteristic.

Quent moved in a private dimension of his own creation. He was, I had no doubt, very much one of the crowd, in the center of it all, but at the same time he had somehow managed to place himself just out of easy reach, perhaps primed for a quick exit. This same potential was also reflected in the way he carried himself, his arms alert at his side, a watchful spring in his gait, ready to turn on a dime.

Although he struck me as being someone who generally enjoyed life in his own sometimes-eccentric way, the two incidents relating to him that I recall most vividly in fact underscored a less open, moodier side. The first involved an outline he had written for a composition; the subjects usually chosen for these essays revolved around sports (how to do the triple jump, rules of baseball) or one's family. Quent's proposed subject was a visit to his uncle's mortuary, and his outline indicated the careful steps through which the composition would progress from a description of the facility, its specific function, the shock of seeing a human body laid out for the first time, and, finally, "Thoughts about death; that it happens to you." The paper, sadly, was never written.

The second incident was more personal. I was walking home from campus one afternoon, and Quent caught sight of me as I passed through the back parking lot of the apartments, and came over to meet me, eventually accompanying me almost as far as my home. He was very preoccupied and told me that his young daughter who was two years old (I hadn't known he was a father) had died some weeks ago in the Tallahassee Memorial Hospital. She had been taken in for some minor surgical procedure, and something had gone wrong. Quent thought she might have had a reaction to medication she had been given, because when he saw her body, "her arms and legs had swollen up, were like balloons." This long stroll up the hill from the apartments on a beautiful spring Florida day made a deep impression on me, not only because what he had to report was so disturbing, but because I was surprised that he had sought me out. The quiet, unaffected manner in which he had told this story left me with some insight into that private dimension in which he seemed to live, and I carried away with me a sense of both his deep weariness and his essential, unexpected gentleness.

Quent Reed came from Panama City, and although no one of his family's name was listed in the telephone directory, I eventually found an old address for his parents. I accepted the friendly offer of a neighbor who happened to be going to Panama City on business to check up on the address, and he returned triumphant, equipped with telephone numbers of mother, sister, cousins.

I called Quent's mother, who referred me to his sister, with whom Quent was apparently living. A little boy answered the phone.

"What color are you?" he asked suspiciously. Taken aback, I at first laughed, but he stubbornly stuck to his guns.

"Are you black or white?" he asked more directly. Taking a cue from my high school days, I replied that I was neither, I was English.

"Quent's right here," the boy responded immediately, "but he's asleep," and he told me I could call back in the afternoon.

I did so, and this time Quent himself came to the phone. I said who I was and asked him if he remembered me.

"Yes, ma'am," he said dully. From word one, this conversation was painfully heavy, and although I plowed determinedly ahead, I learned little more than that Quent was working full time at Hardee's as a cook, and that he had recently been to Tallahassee to take "the mother of his children" to the Tallahassee Memorial Hospital. Finally, I came to the point and asked Quent if he would allow me to interview him.

"Yes, ma'am," he said, his voice expressing the hard resignation of someone used to obeying orders, and not a spark of interest. Nonetheless, I made an arrangement to call him back at the end of the summer, when his job at Hardee's would have ended, to set up an appointment. I hung up the telephone deeply discouraged. I recognized no one I had ever known in that beaten voice.

When I did call a month or so later, it was now his sister who answered, and who told me that Quent was no longer living with her—he was in prison.

"For, you know, his parole," she said vaguely. But she had the name of the prison and was helpful about giving me telephone numbers and addresses. And after several talks with the appropriate authorities, I received permission to meet with Quentin Reed at River Junction Correctional Institute, outside of Chattahoochee, about half an hour's drive from Tallahassee.

It was December, a time of year that in North Florida can be either mild and balmy, as it had been when I visited Orson, or wild and wintery, as it was now. The foliage had only just, at this late date, begun to turn a muted autumnal red. Chattahoochee is best known locally for its mental institution, and when I was a child one would taunt a person by saying "You belong in Chattahoochee."

River Junction Correctional Institute lay outside the small town, positioned on a hill that sloped up from the Chattahoochee road, like a stockade on a lookout bluff. It was untamed country here, with old oaks and uncut forest banking the agitated gray Chattahoochee River some distance below. The "institute" itself, big brick buildings and barbed-wire coils, was unmistakably a prison; but paradoxically, its hill-slope lawn was crowded with formally placed blue metal chairs, which had they accommodated actual prisoners might have lent an imposing, grave air to the scene, but vacant as they were curiously suggested some abandoned antique social event—lawn tennis, perhaps, or a bandstand picnic.

Stepping through the lobby of the main building, I gave my name and identification to a female guard behind a glass security window. Beyond the door separating the lobby from the facility proper, another heavy door slammed. Shortly, a male guard appeared behind the window, then came out to unlock the separating door, gesturing for me to follow him through to a spartan room opening onto a corridor, in the center of which were three tables and some chairs. Another door slammed again and suddenly Quent appeared ahead of a second guard who, as they drew abreast of me, turned Quent to face the corridor wall so as to frisk him. He appeared shorter than I had remembered him, not so much taller than me, although it may be that his baggy blue prison garb gave the illusion of stunting him. When Quent turned back, he was looking directly at me, but his face remained impassive, and I too found myself reluctant to reveal anything of what I was thinking. The guard conducted him into the room, searched him again, and then indicated that Quent and I could sit down at the table. He himself took up a position by the door, a short distance away.

"Hello, Quent," I said, finding myself unexpectedly at ease once we were seated. Now that I could actually look at him, I realized I had in fact been looking forward to seeing him.

He shook my hand. "Now I recognize you," he said and smiled; or rather, one tooth glinted between his lips; I had forgotten this smile, so characteristic—friendly, but not excessive; secretive, protective.

"Yes ma'am," he said again, as he had during our earlier telephone conversation, in answer to some question I asked at the beginning of the interview, but my face must have registered alarm, for the tooth suddenly glinted again and he said apologetically, "Just habit."

"What are you actually here for?" I asked. "I know you broke parole, but I didn't have the nerve to ask your family what the parole was for."

"Armed robbery. And I didn't break parole; I turned myself in," he said, one eye looking steadily at me, the other off to the wall.

After his abrupt departure from Florida State in 1983, Quent had sat out a year, working in Panama City, and then gone to Valdosta State College in Georgia, for three years, on a football scholarship arranged by his old coach from Mosley High School. In his junior year, he was stopped by a back injury: "I hit someone the wrong way in a play. My back still bothers me; it never went away."

Quent had been told when he last checked that he was ninety-five hours short of graduation from Valdosta State. (Ninety-five hours!? Two years at Florida State, three years at Valdosta and still two years short of graduation for an undergraduate degree in education?)

"When I left Valdosta, I came back to Panama City, and got a job through connections, you know, because I know the place. This is where I grew up." The job Quent obtained through his connections was as a cook at Captain Anderson's Restaurant, where he worked seventy hours for three hundred and fifty dollars a week for the next three years.

"I loved high school. I believed in doing my work, and fun came second. It was something to do. If I stayed home, there would be work to do—housework, things like that. High school gave me a reason to get out. I liked mathematics; yes, I seemed pretty good at it. I was pretty good with numbers. In high school, there was one good teacher, Mrs. Bailey; she stayed on me, made me stick with it, that far anyway. And there was one black teacher I really admired. Miss Oates. Typing teacher. She told people what you needed to know about how to make it out there. She didn't hold anything back. She was very, very respected. High school teachers were pretty much students themselves; they tried to learn about us. They know their subject, they teach a bit, but then they try to observe us. I had the basic English courses, but there was no real reading. In high school, I thought I was pretty average in reading, pretty average in English."

It was when he came to Florida State that he discovered that the level he had obtained was not in fact "pretty average." There was chapter after chapter to read, and he could not do it.

"We had never read in high school. When I got to college, I had never heard of an adverb or an adjective. I can't spell that well, and I can't pronounce words right. You know, I would like to learn to write more, I would like—right now, I use little words; if I could write more, I would read more, and I would use bigger words, I would use more complicated words, and I would say things correctly.

"How much have I written since I left college? Nothing, zero, zip. I write two times a month at the most, you know, letters home. There are some people here that can read; they're the ones that write letters, or do legal work for you, though usually for a price. No, I was not educated from high school. They really didn't care if we learned or not in high school; I thought college would be different.

"I wish I knew more history and more biology, or science as we called it back then; it's important. We need all this, to learn about the world. Learn more about other people; I only recently found out that Columbus didn't discover America the way I had always been taught; there were Indians in America—how could he discover it? I guess they mean he was the first American to discover America."

In the corridor outside, a prisoner went by, dressed in the blue inmate's uniform that resembled pajamas (compared to which Billy's white uniform now looked, in retrospect, like a flashy tracksuit) and chains around his wrists and ankles. He seemed in good spirits for all the metal he was carrying, cheerfully poking his head into the interview room to see what was going on before being moved along by the accompanying guard. I couldn't decide at that moment whether everything I had been interested in asking Quent was completely fatuous and beside every point, or was, after all, the point itself. Facing Quent across the table where he sat with his shoulders squared, very proud, although obedient and cooperative, I found myself thinking that I was not at that moment remotely interested in his high school, or his spelling, or his experience at F.S.U. What I wanted to know was how he was bearing up, what he would do when he got out, if

there was any means of unsnarling what I was only now beginning to discern as the terrible chaos of his life. I had so far resisted asking the obvious question, namely the circumstances of
the criminal charges against him, and knew that this was mostly
because I liked him too much to want to know. I had an over-
whelming sense that I had never before been with so essentially
isolated a person, and I think I would have had this sense even
had our interview not been held in prison; that if I had caught up
with him over the summer during his off hour from Hardee's, I
would have come away with the same deep impression of his un-
connectedness. It is impossible for me to determine the specific
factors that I found so affecting—certainly they didn't lie in anything he had so far said. The leaden sound of his voice over the
telephone when I had spoken to him in the summer had first cau-
tioned me that life for him was not going particularly well. And
I knew at the outset of our interview that he would not petition
me to help him, or foresee ways in which contact with me could
be of some practical use. Such overtures entail certain, even minimal, expectations, and I now saw that he had none.

At Mosley High School, Quent had run track, played basketball, and was one of the first two black athletes on the tennis
team. "But," he said, "football was the only way in. Most black
people don't read when they're young; they do sports instead.
You know, everybody is looking for their idol—my idol was
O. J. Simpson—you know, when you try to find an idol, try to
find someone to be like somebody else? In high school, sports
was all I did; I played sports and I went to school.

"I was a running back in high school, but I played defensive
corner at F.S.U. I was recruited by Coach Shaw, who was the defensive line coach. No, I was never thinking of the pros. For me,
when I came to F.S.U., education was first, football was second;
no, I was there for the education. My father stressed that education came first."

Quent has a brother and a sister who attended Gulf Coast
Community College, the brother lasting longest, for some two

years. Most of his family—his mother, stepfather, four brothers, and two sisters—live in Panama City, although one brother is in the service, in Germany.

"When I first came to F.S.U., I thought the facilities were great; I didn't go so far afield from campus. In terms of setting the classes at F.S.U., it was very limited because it had to be between eight in the morning and one in the afternoon, and usually they wanted you to get some of those basic courses, so they set your schedule; you could always come back, though, and say what you liked, or didn't like—you would have that kind of feedback; but the first schedule was going to be set by what people thought would fit in that time frame and be easy.

"Looking back now, I would have liked to have majored in communications and gone into broadcasting. I was not clear at that point in time what I wanted to major in. There were lots of distractions. There were drugs and so on. No, the coaches didn't know; it was a thing kept between the players. A lot of people did it; some did it, some didn't. But I wanted to be with the crowd. I wanted to be one of those at that time.

"In my community, where you grew up, there was a lack of vision. You graduate from high school, get a job, and make babies. The big difference that I noticed when I was at F.S.U. was that blacks were just there to be there, just wanted to be there, to say they went to college, or they were there for the sport, or to party. Whites wanted to learn, wanted to be like their parents, to graduate.

"I was never on academic probation. I was at Florida State from 1981 till 1983, and I had a 2.6 to 2.7 average. I needed to study more harder, and think of sports second; but in reality football is first and education is second. There is no way round that, once you accept a football scholarship. At that time, I wasn't concentrating, I couldn't think. There were a lot of distractions. Just living too fast, I was just living too fast.

"When my child died, in 1981—it was a cleft-palate operation. Me and the mother of the child had filed suit with a lawyer in

Tallahassee, Mr. Jefferson, but we dropped it. I think the mother settled, received some settlement for this. I left Monday for the funeral. I called Coach Bowden I was going. We had a bowl game coming up and he didn't want me to take time off, but I went for the funeral and stayed through Sunday. I came back to take my exams, but I knew I was in trouble. And then I just left.

"I felt I was running away from the problem. I was doing something that was difficult for me. Being over my head—just not wanting to study. It was difficult, and I was not enjoying football. I didn't like Tallahassee; it didn't work out for me. It wasn't for me—I really didn't want to go—the surroundings in Tallahassee, the drugs, life was just too fast for me. I came back for finals, but I knew I was in trouble.

"When I went to Valdosta, I majored in education for high schools. If I would have finished, probably I'd be teaching P.E. in high school somewhere. I like working with kids. I love them, as a matter of fact. Parents nowadays don't care if their kids get in trouble or not; the young guys now don't go to school, they just hang out. I guess they're just afraid of it.

"If it were me, I'd open up a club, right there in the neighborhood. Tell the parents to bring their kids. I'd have games, I'd have food, I'd have their minds . . . I'd have their minds occupied, I'd try and have teachers come in. We'd have media programs, reading, writing, talking, which we particularly need in black neighborhoods."

"Why do you need a club? Why can't this work in the high school itself?" I asked.

"No, no, no," he said adamantly, his face becoming animated. "Because in high school, the parents think their kids are going to high school, they expect the teachers to be doing the discipline. If parents think their kids are in school, they expect the teachers to be doing the disciplining of the kids. If a teacher needs to communicate with a parent about how the kids are not in school, letters get intercepted in the mail and phone calls get intercepted—the parent may never know the kid isn't there, if they are just too busy or they don't care enough to ask. If you had a club with young kids and parents, they would have to know what was happening. A neighbor would tell the parent that their kid hadn't turned up.

"My generation, the kind of thing we'd do is hang out, drink beer, drink wine at night, drinking wine at nighttime—but you had to be in school. The parents checked and found out. Parents today are so much younger that they don't know what parenthood is all about."

I asked the question I most wanted answered. "What," I said, "will you do when you get out?"

"I'm going to go back to my family, and I'm going to talk to my children. I have four kids, age ten, six, three, and two, by a lady I was with for seven years. We're not together anymore. I'm going to go to the unemployment and get a job through them; they try and have something set up for you when you get out of here.

"In here, we have drug rehabilitation and N.A. rehabilitation, which is not smoking, and alcohol rehabilitation; but that's it, there's no instruction. Although there are courses for people who haven't finished high school, there is nothing for people that have already gone beyond that. No, no instruction whatsoever. We don't really have counselors; no, we have a psychiatrist and we have some sort of supervisor. I spend my time working in the laundry, doing some kind of exercise, reading the Bible, just lying in bed, or watching videos. We have tournaments, Ping-Pong tournaments, things like that."

I gave in to the urge to give Quent a little lecture, about productive use of leisure time for self-enhancement, about reading, getting in practice again, about studying anything at all, perhaps through correspondence courses.

"I got to ask you to leave for lunch now," said the guard at the door suddenly. My arrangement with the authorities for this interview had entailed conducting it in two sessions. Swiftly, Quent and I were escorted in our two opposite directions, and I found myself walking freely into the windy, wild day outside.

I took a drive up to a lookout point over the river, then along a road that dipped and rolled on hills elevated above the red-gold treetops undulating below. I found a pleasant local diner for lunch, populated at this hour by mostly obese white people. Having ordered tea and a sandwich, I looked around me, wondering what it would be like to grow up in a small southern town like this, so remote from everything going on in the world. . . .

"Howz yer sister?" I heard a man ask his friend at the adjacent table, and he replied that she was fine, just fine and really enjoying her current work, which was restructuring the economy of Lithuania, following which they embarked upon a detailed conversation about the enduring problems of Baltic politics.

I arrived back at the institute at two o'clock as planned and was led at once into the interview room, where Quent was already waiting. A noticeable change had taken place in his demeanor; he was up, confident, and his hard-set expression had softened.

"I don't need to ask my supervisor about any correspondence courses," he said right away, the words tumbling out. "I'm going to ask Mr. Mitchell; he teaches at the Gulf Coast Community College and my mother knows him. He lives on the same street as us. He'll get me the information, and he can get my records from Valdosta.

"I came back in Panama City again—this is 1988. Nineteen eighty-eight was the year I was arrested, in Panama City. I was out drinking and partying. We went by a store to get some beer. My friend went into the store and I came in after him, and as I came through the door he said 'Get back in the car.' I had a burnt on my chest," said Quent, rubbing his shirt. "I had a burnt from a radiator boiling up on me and I had my shirt off because of this burnt on my chest, and that's what they recognized. The clerk said it was me. The police came down to the beach where I was standing by a car drinking a beer—the other guy had already gone on into the club. They recognized the car and asked me had I been there, and they took me back with them and the clerk identified me and said I was one of the men. They knew there was another one, but they never found him. I never told on him. They made it clear to me that I was going to be in the system; it was just cleaner for me to say that I did it and get fifteen years on paper. My case was represented by a public defender. No, she was no good. She didn't do a good job. She was overloaded—this was about Christmastime; she said there was no evidence and did I just want to get out? So I took fifteen years on paper; I did six and a half years on the outside, I'll do two good years in here, which counts as four good years on parole; it's like two for one, so when I get out of this I'll have four more years to report. I had to report once a month to my probation officer; it's a drag. I turned myself in; I just got tired of doing it. This is the only time I've been in trouble, the only time. My parents were very upset. My brother spent some time in prison. I never asked what for; I figured if he wanted me to know, he'd tell me. He never did, so I guess he was ashamed."

I wanted to know about the friend, the one who had gotten away, whom he hadn't told on.

Quent's eyes narrowed.

"His time will come," he said very softly. "His luck will change. The way he's going now, his luck will change. We don't talk anymore, we don't even communicate."

There was a pause.

"Why," I asked with sudden exasperation, "did you hang out with these people, with people who use drugs in Tallahassee, which you didn't like, with people who carry guns? It's all very well for you to say you run with the crowd, but isn't there a point where you just rebel? Just want to cut loose?"

"That's what I did," he countered with some passion. "That's what I did in my second year in Tallahassee; I just didn't want any more of it. I left, and came back to Panama City and pulled myself together.

"If you grow up around drugs, drugs are all you know; if everyone around you is doing one thing, then that is going to be what you know and you are not going to judge people by it. You are going to want to still be like them—you're still going to want to try it. You don't look to school to give you the values, you look to be like your friends. When I relax, people I party with are only going to be people that I know. People don't think of being themselves; you don't think to be like yourself. *Now* I can know myself, now, but it's taken to this time.

"Everybody, everybody I know carried guns. Everybody. *I* never carried a gun; I have never owned one. I hate them. I will not touch them. I've been threatened; I've been shot at. When I was in Valdosta, I was at a party, and I was going out of the party and I trod on this guy's foot by the door; it was crowded, I didn't know I'd done it. He came out, said some words to me. Then he started shooting." He paused reflectively. "Well, I guess it's something to do with the fact that I was going with his girl-friend," he conceded, the tooth glinting. "I ran around the corner and got into a car and went away. The incident was reported and I was questioned, and I told the cops who did it."

"Didn't you worry about what the man you told on might do to you?"

"Naw, he was a coward. A man who would hide behind a gun is a coward; he's too scared to fight."

"Scared or not, he's still got a gun; he can do things."

"Naw, he's got a lot to lose. If he killed me, he'd get caught; he'd end up in jail," said Quent, with no apparent sense of irony. "He thought about it and he let it go.

"The only other time that I was threatened, I was out of town—this is in Panama City—with some friends, driving off to another town, looking for girls and partying. We ended up in an-other neighborhood where they knew we're out of town and one of them just pulled out a gun, and he just hold it there. We just left right away."

"What do you do when somebody threatens you with a gun?"

"Try to talk him down, tell him not to do that. Tell him about the time he's going to do in prison for a little simple argument, for something about a woman."

"Why have you never had a gun, if everyone you know has one?"

"Guns? What do I need them for? I don't need it for protection. There are a lot of people out there with problems and they are going to try and take it out on somebody else. I just want to stay away from troubles; you just want to stay away from trouble. You can't get caught up in their troubles; you have to strive on, look forward to the future, not get caught up. Just strive on to the future.

"Kids where I grew up, they try to be as we call it hard; and they're not really hard, they're either lazy, they're trying to find an easy way out. They look around and they see even older people dealing drugs. Forty percent stay in it; they may do other work, they may do other jobs, but they are still selling drugs. Sometimes it's in the blood; they love it, they like the danger. They like it until someone puts a stop to it. Black youth don't really know about setting goals for the future. I got to learn about setting goals too late. People—we don't set goals. We live from day to day. Most people where I grew up rely on welfare; the young ladies are happy with welfare—that takes care of them, or child support, and then there is no planning; there's no need to plan ahead.

"Yeah, you could bring in other role models—businessmen, ministers, but no cops. We would let him talk, but we won't pay any attention to him. We know that he's trying to do right. He's out there trying to do right and you know it. Educated people, if they were well educated they were, you know, high class, they were respected, but not as role models. People don't see the way you get there. It's not the same as being a sports hero, which everybody understands. You respect them, but you're not associated with them. I knew one guy who went to school with me; he ended up taking remedial courses too. He got in a reading class but he didn't and he couldn't keep up with it; he said he didn't need it and I said 'Take the remedial work'; but our friends told him—'You're wasting your time. You're wasting your parents' money, you're getting college debts. You'll owe the college something'—and they talked him into quitting.

"Ninety-five percent of role models are sports heroes. You don't know that many blacks doing well outside of sports. Yes, there's a black entertainment station on television; I didn't watch much television, because I was always working. I know the station; there's black music and some black programs, but nothing that would bring in people you would not have heard about doing more serious work.

"It's not that the black family's not strong. The families are still strong. It's just people don't get married. Some reason—some lady might see someone out there that she wants; same reason that I might see someone that turns me on. Black people don't believe in marriage." He glinted. "Maybe we don't believe that we have that much time left—we might be shot in the next minute; but I believe that for every one of us that dies there're two black kids born. Kids get lots of attention, even in the broken homes; lots of care. They are the strength of our community, they are our future. Kids are important." As on each occasion that he spoke of children, Quent's entire manner changed—his eyes glowed, he leaned forward, he gestured with his hands, completely absorbed in what he was saying.

"Neighborhoods wouldn't be neighborhoods, they wouldn't be the same without the kids, without the noise, without their playing. They're good kids—they go to school up to a certain age; the problems start with adolescence. Parents can't stop work to look after them and often the father is absent so the mother's out there working. Parents can't just stop work when they've got trouble with one kid, because they've got other kids to feed.

"I would need a job when I get out of here. I'd get my own place and go from there. That's all. That's all I need. I can make it. You know what you have to do when you get out of here; you've got to get a job. Otherwise you have to do the next best thing, because there is a family to feed.

"I can say I have one friend, one real friend, in the last seven years. He's in pretty much the same situation that I'm in. He was inside, only for drugs. He's on the right track now. He has four kids too. I take the kids every summer and I get to have them on the weekends, and we take our kids to the park, play games, take them to movies, or have something to eat, you know, then we go home and maybe just talk. I'll drink a beer and watch TV. That's our routine. I'm thirty-one years old. We're not getting any younger; I'm thirty-one years old, he's thirty-eight. We're getting older—we both figured that out.

"I figure out that by the age of fifty I'll have everything that I would need by then." He laughed again. "If I don't have my degree by then, I guess I won't need it.

"My mother is watching the kids now. Their mother, she has some kind of disease. She can't walk anymore; she's losing the use of her hands. We are no longer seeing each other; we haven't really been together for five or six years. We don't talk to each other; we argue with each other. We don't say—'You're doing a good job with the kids.' All we do is argue at each other. I don't know what it is; that's the way she seems to want it.

"I may end up with the kids. I would love that. I love the kids, period. I want to give them a future. I want them to know—'You can go to school; you don't have to do sports. If you want to do sports, and that's the way you want to do it, you can, but you don't have to do sports. We can work on it. You might have to work, you might have to take a year off to work, you might have to take a course and come back, but we can work it out.' I'll do some things that my mother and father didn't do for me. Like ask them questions. 'What did you *learn* today in school?' If they didn't learn anything, I'll say, 'Go get your books. Learn something now and then come and tell me about it.' This summer, I had my young one at the table, writing, learning how to write his name, and I had the other kid in the back room reading a book; he wanted to go out and play, but I said 'You stay there and read.' I try and get him to read about a chapter a day.

"You said you didn't want to lecture me," he said, suddenly changing subjects. "But over lunch, I went back, and I was thinking about what you said about doing something here. It made me feel good that there was someone who cared."

The circumstances of our interview had thrust a kind of terrible intimacy upon us. For my own part, I had felt a kind of conspiratorial alliance with Quent when he had first entered the interview room, and I did not think he would receive many other visitors over the years. His situation did not compare with that of Billy Allen, who operated in a bigger world, and who would always charm and persuade and have "contacts." What I perceived to be Quent's genuine needs seemed so very minimal—a place to live and a job adequate to care for his children—that I felt a kind of terror in recognizing that they might not ever be met.

The guard by the door had signaled that I was overstaying.

"Do you have anything you want to get off your chest?" I asked, as quietly as I could.

The tooth glinted, and he pressed his hands to his chest.

"No, I got it off."

Acknowledgments

In addition to all the players and their families who graciously agreed to participate in this project, I owe thanks to the following people for their help and support: Will Faye, Linda Jones, Dr. Brian Mand, and the F.S.U. Football Office; my editors, Bob Gottlieb and George Andreou; my agent, Anthony Sheil; my sister, Joanna; my good friends Laura Slatkin, Jan Mitchell, and George Butler; and Mr. Woytych, Mr. Scott, Mr. Edwards, and Colonel Hartenstien, the immigration officers whose help allowed my family to remain in this country.

A Note on the Type

The text of this book was set in Simoncini Garamond, a modern version by Francesco Simoncini of the type attributed to the famous Parisian type cutter Claude Garamond (c. 1480–1561). Garamond was a pupil of Geoffroy Tory and is believed to have based his letters on the Venetian models, although he introduced a number of important differences, and it is to him that we owe the letter we know as old style. He gave to his letters a certain elegance and a feeling of movement that won for their creator an immediate reputation and the patronage of Francis I of France.

Composed by ComCom, Allentown, Pennsylvania. Printed and bound by The Haddon Craftsmen, an R. R. Donnelley & Sons company, Scranton, Pennsylvania

Designed by Anthea Lingeman